100 THINGS TO DO IN JUPITER BEFORE YOU DIE

Players negotiate the 16th hole of The Bear Trap.
Photo courtesy of The Honda Classic

100 THINGS TO DO IN JUPITER BEFORE YOU DIE

AMY WOODS

REEDY PRESS

Reedy Press
PO Box 5131
St. Louis, MO 63139, USA
www.reedypress.com

Library of Congress Control Number: 2023937950

ISBN: 9781681064642

Design by Jill Halpin

Cover photo by Brian “Harooki” Lee

Printed in the United States of America
26 27 5 4 3

DEDICATION

To the authors in my life
who encouraged—and inspired—me to become one

Joe Namath enjoys The Broadway Burger at Lucky Shuck.
Photo courtesy of Jessica Namath

CONTENTS

Music and Entertainment

Sports and Recreation

Culture and History

Evelyn & Arthur
Photo courtesy of Amy Woods

PREFACE

My old boyfriend used a great expression whenever he and I headed out for a long walk on the beach, a slow drive down A1A, a cool concert in the amphitheater, boat drinks with our besties, or any of the endless events to which we received invites. In so many words, it was to figuratively "suck the nectar" out of everything we did. And why not?

When you live in an area rife with food and drink, music and entertainment, sports and recreation, culture and history, and shopping and fashion (the five chapters of *100 Things to Do in Jupiter Before You Die*), golden opportunities present themselves day in and day out. I aimed to "suck the nectar" out of them, living, laughing, and loving as much as possible each step of the way.

I have climbed to the top of the Jupiter Inlet Lighthouse lots of times, and the view still mesmerizes me. I have kayaked the "Wild and Scenic" Loxahatchee River again and again, and the feeling of being a million miles away from civilization gives me a repeated rush. I have seen my share of shows at the Maltz Jupiter Theatre, and the stage keeps getting better with age. Nothing beats a starry night at Square Grouper Tiki Bar. Shakespeare by the Sea and the Palm Beach Holiday Boat Parade are only-in-South-Florida types of occasions I never miss. The Jupiter Riverwalk and Harbourside Place are meant to be explored, and when I do either, I do both.

During the process of writing the book, I learned that goat yoga makes you giggle, that drinking while painting is therapeutic, and that going to a Spring Training game is sort of like watching history in the making. I learned that not enough of us know about the impact Burt Reynolds had on the town or about the impact the town had on the movie star. I learned that we should celebrate the success of Charlie & Joe's at Love Street and how the tasteful—and tasty—venture by "Broadway" Joe Namath is shaping the future of the funky fishing village.

100 Things to Do in Jupiter Before You Die is an ode to the incredible experiences I have had and a primer for the ones awaiting you. I aspired to illustrate the beauty, enjoyment, and magic that Jupiter and its neighboring communities offer. I endeavored to dispense bits of background for context and to add a little intrigue to the items on the list. In the end, my goal was to share the reasons why setting aside time for frivolity and fun as well as for moments more poignant and provocative is so important in life. I am hopeful that, after reading the book, you, too, decide to "suck the nectar" out of everything you do.

ACKNOWLEDGMENTS

It takes a village to write a book, and in the case of *100 Things to Do in Jupiter Before You Die*, it took two villages, two towns, one city, and a county. Thank you to the caring, kind, and understanding employees and volunteers of Jupiter, Tequesta, Juno Beach, Palm Beach Gardens, North Palm Beach, and Palm Beach County for returning my calls, replying to emails, and meeting with me. Your interest in my project enabled me to turn concepts into copy.

Appreciation also is in order for those who talked to me, answered my questions, offered advice, suggested things for the book, and gave me tours of some of the places that appear on the pages ahead. In addition to André, Enid, Deeawn, Dennis, Jody, Ritchey, Robyn, Todd, and Tom, a shout out is in order for Tamra, who sacrificed a Sunday afternoon to show me around VIP-style.

Thank you to everyone who supplied photos for the book, because a picture truly is worth 1,000 words.

Thank you to my Gold Coast PR Council family, who continues to help me grow professionally and personally.

To the many girlfriends who, throughout my labor of love, checked in on me, delivered words of wisdom and wit, and dragged me away from my desk as needed—I could not have done it without you.

Last but not least, credit needs to be given to my brother Jimmy for his relentless support and to my cousin Adam, who, after a few hot toddies one Thanksgiving, called me from New Jersey and told me I really, really need to write a book about South Florida.

Photo courtesy of Feast of Little Italy

FOOD AND DRINK

1

HEAD TO THE HEART OF JUPITER
AT CHARLIE & JOE'S AT LOVE STREET

When Pro Football Hall of Fame legend Joe Namath opened Charlie & Joe's at Love Street, the venue rekindled Jupiter's funky fishing village flame. Memories of the rope swing and the swing bridge, of bonfires on the beach and beach barbecues, and of the old marina and bait shop linger at the enchanting escape in the town's true core. The new waterfront destination features four diverse restaurants—Beacon, Topside at the Beacon, Lucky Shuck Oyster Bar & Taphouse, and The Tacklebox Jupiter Seafood & Supply Co.—a working boat dock, and picturesque views of the iconic lighthouse. An adventurous array of water activities—eco-touring, e-foiling, kayaking, paddleboarding, and romantic cruising aboard the *Love Boat*—salute the nautical lifestyle of generations of locals. Namath, along with corporate partner Charlie Modica, have cemented Jupiter's place on the map by reimagining the area as a charming and festive food experience.

1116 Love St., 561-532-3280
lovestreetjupiter.com

HERE IS WHAT TO EXPECT AT EACH OF THE CHARLIE & JOE'S AT LOVE STREET RESTAURANTS

Beacon

Fine dining indoors and outdoors centered around an exhibition kitchen theatrically showcasing American fare with Mediterranean flare

561-532-3280

thebeaconjupiter.com

Topside at the Beacon

A rooftop lounge where small plates, big drinks, and a resident DJ spinning it old-school can while away the day and night

561-532-3270

topsidejupiter.com

Lucky Shuck Oyster Bar & Taphouse

Gulf Coast eclecticism (i.e., macadamia- and pecan-crusted fish and grits), New Orleans libations (cheers to the Royal Street Saz), and, of course, football

561-532-3331

luckyshuckjupiter.com

The Tacklebox Jupiter Seafood & Supply Co.

Great for breakfast or lunch on the go with egg sandwiches and poke bowls or for picking up provisions for dinner at home

561-532-3332

tackleboxjupiter.com

2

PARTY FOR THE POOCHES

AT THE FRIENDS OF JUPITER BEACH FOOD & WINE FESTIVAL

An awesome afternoon of nibbles and nips comes to town each spring, raising money for a nonprofit whose mission entails keeping a dog-friendly section of shore clean and well-maintained. The Friends of Jupiter Beach Food & Wine Festival usually sells out, so make sure to get your tickets early. More than two dozen of the area's best restaurants set up stations in a hidden plaza beneath the Indiantown Road drawbridge, a pretty cool, nicely shaded scene for a shindig. Samples of delectable items are paper-plated up throughout the day, from surf to turf to vegetarian, as wine corks work their way out of bottles at every turn. And there is live music with which to wash it all down. The festival is the biggest benefit of the year for the Friends of Jupiter Beach, and canines are welcome to wag their tails at the affair.

Plaza Down Under the Riverwalk
25 S Coastal Way, 561-748-8140
friendsofjupiterbeach.org

3

CHOW DOWN LIKE A CHAMPION

AT THE WOODS JUPITER

Arguably the most famous name in golf, Tiger Woods lives, works, and plays in Jupiter. The local legend has five Masters victories, four PGA Tour Championship wins, and three titles apiece in the US Open and the British Open. As Woods's legacy on the course continues, he also is making an impression off of it. His restaurant, The Woods Jupiter, debuted in 2015. A boisterous sports bar on game days, it was designed as a destination for family and friends to socialize and satiate. The focus remains on food that fuels the body. Among the eponymous dishes are The Woods Burger, The Woods Rack of Ribs, and The Woods Signature Mac and Cheese. The Woods Herb & Honey Bread is a best bet for brunch, and The Woods House Salad scores serious lunch points. And you never know—the man himself might be in the house.

Harbourside Place
129 Soundings Ave., 561-320-9627
thewoods.tigerwoods.com

4

MOVE, GROOVE, WINE, AND DINE
AT GUANABANAS

No visit to Jupiter is complete without an epicurean escape to Guanabanas, pronounced *gwuh-NAH-buh-nuhs.* Named after the spiny soursop fruit indigenous to the Caribbean, the lushly landscaped oasis on an oxbow of the Loxahatchee River looks like a piece of paradise. You enter by crossing a whimsical wooden footbridge that leads to shaded nooks filled with hightops and lowtops. There, you can dine in *al fresco* serenity. For a little more action, you can wait for a table near the secluded stage where local, regional, and national acts—Julian Marley, Mishka, and Rob Thomas, to name a few—perform. Other features that augment the sensation of stealing away to a secret hideaway are coquina-stone pathways, fragrant flowers, sultry nighttime lighting, and a tranquil boardwalk. Settle in with a Lime in the Coconut cocktail and a tray of Florida Gulf steamers to appreciate the ambience.

960 N A1A, 561-747-8878
guanabanas.com

5

ENJOY ECLECTIC EDIBLES
AT 1000 NORTH

When a bunch of sports stars led by Michael Jordan premiere a restaurant, you can expect the menu will reflect the fanfare. At 1000 North, discerning diners can feast on Wagyu steaks and Delmonico rib eyes or splurge on the rack of lamb or the Dover sole. Modern American pleasures—truffle salt fries with butter and garlic, tavern chips with blue cheese and smoked bacon, and pimento cheese toast with ham and tomatoes—emerge from the kitchen and into a slick setting that resembles a cruise ship. If the brass and wood accents and subtle lighting do not make you feel as if you are out at sea, sweeping views of the Loxahatchee River will. Meals also can be taken at the bar or on the terrace. 1000 North operates as a private club, too, with members receiving access to the exclusive second-story lounge where MJ likes to hang.

1000 N US Hwy. 1, 561-570-1000
1000north.com

6

NOSH
AT TOOJAY'S

South Florida, and the state as a whole, is synonymous with several things—Disney World, Ponce de Leon, Publix, and TooJay's. Known for its amusing avian mascot outfitted in a chef's hat and apron, the New York–style deli has a loyal following. The restaurant boasts nearly two dozen locations on the peninsula, and one of them is Jupiter. Its scratch-made soups, high-piled sandwiches, chopped salads, coveted black-and-white cookies, and to-die-for Killer Cake likely will make you a repeat customer. Try the traditional brisket, a meal of lean beef and potato pancakes topped with a mushroom glaze, or the Lox of Love grilled cream cheese on rye with salmon, pickled cucumbers, and dill mayonnaise. For an appetizer, go for the TooJay's Famous Knish filled with spinach. Lunch and dinner deals are available throughout the week, and every Wednesday, half-price bottles of wine make an appearance.

4050 US Hwy. 1, 561-627-5555
toojays.com

7

TEMPT YOUR TASTE BUDS AT BRICK & BARREL GASTRO PUB

As its name implies, Brick & Barrel Gastro Pub oozes American urbanism. Inside the industrial walls of the bold—yet at the same time, boutique—3,000-square-foot setting, you will find something to crave. The scratch kitchen specializes in craft cuisine, and the dark, aged spirits behind the bar not only are shaken and stirred but also smoked. Will you choose the Jupiter "Jerk" Wings or the venison osso buco? What about the classic slider or the Florida lobster roll? There are plenty of possibilities for pescatarians (salmon and shrimp among them) and for vegetarians (the mushroom risotto, roasted squash salad, and Supper Club Crudité to name a few). Live music takes the stage several times each week, and when you listen from your svelte seat with a Brick's House Old Fashioned in hand, it makes lunch or dinner out all the merrier.

Abacoa Town Center
1153 Town Center Dr., 561-623-0916
brickandbarrelpub.com

FALL IN LOVE AT FIRST BITE
AT DUNE DOG CAFÉ

The tin roof, thatched overhang, and wood-plank floor set the mood. The multipage menu's mouthwatering descriptions cast the pickup line. The top-notch tube steaks sweep you off your feet. Before you know it, you are crooning and swooning over The Naked Dog, a Hebrew National number on a grilled New England roll. More than 10 types of hot dogs are ready and waiting to steal your heart at Dune Dog Café. Whether you choose Chicago, chili, or corn, you inevitably will find yourself shamelessly cheating on all of them. Because who can resist Leroy Brown's Junkyard Dog, a mess of melted cheese, spicy sauce, and diced onions? The tropical shack also prepares award-winning burgers; The Cabbage Patch is covered in coleslaw, pickles, and Thousand Island dressing, and The Big Kahuna is a half-pounder basted in bacon and barbecue sauce. Ribs, salads, sandwiches, and seafood specials add to the allure.

775 N Alt. A1A, 561-744-6667
dunedog.com

TIP

The come-as-you-are atmosphere of Dune Dog Café makes it a superb lunch stop after a morning at the beach or a mellow happy hour hangout in the early evening. Be sure to get a picture of yourself smirking through the surfing mascot's face-in-the-hole board.

REALIZE YOU NEED COFFEE

AT I NEED COFFEE

The casual and cozy storefront that opens bright and early sells freshly roasted gourmet blends so aromatic you might catch a buzz after one whiff. The small-but-mighty shop proudly prefers Haitian Blue Mountain over the highly touted Jamaican Blue Mountain label that has become the gold standard for our morning mug. Its Singing Rooster brand of beans brews a bold beverage that will make you want to come back for another dose the next day. The South Florida–by-way–of-central Illinois owners also supply luscious Haitian chocolate and collectible Haitian art. Hot, made-to-order breakfast sandwiches, egg bites, sausage biscuits, and pastries of all varieties are available, too. Grab an airy table by the window or plop down on a sofa in the corner as you nurse your way to nirvana. If you are pressed for time, take your liquid lightning in a toter.

711 W Indiantown Rd., 561-401-9092
ineedcoffeejupiter.com

WHY PICK STARBUCKS WHEN YOU ARE IN A TOWN AS COFFEE-CRAZED AS JUPITER? HERE ARE TWO LOCAL CHOICES

Oceana Coffee

A husband-and-wife-owned shop

150 US Hwy. 1, Tequesta, 561-768-7887

221 Old Dixie Hwy., Tequesta, 561-401-2453

oceanacoffee.com

Subculture Coffee

A shop centered on good, kind treatment

107 Front St., 561-320-6005

11701 Lake Victoria Gardens Ave., Palm Beach Gardens

561-323-7756

subculturecoffee.com

10

FIND THE GOURMAND IN YOU
AT FOOD TRUCK FRIDAYS

A culinary carnival converges on Abacoa Town Center once a month when as many as two dozen wheeled kitchens pull up streetside and put it in park for the night. One of them prepares pepperoni pizza pinwheels baked until golden brown. You alternatively can opt for the vegetarian version filled with spinach or the lasagna version stuffed with sausage. Another one busts out bowls of gooey macaroni and cheese topped with brisket, lobster, or pulled pork. Meathead's BBQ smokes racks of ribs and smothers chicken in thick, tangy sauce. Choose from *carne asada*, chorizo, or shrimp-and-avocado tacos at Tacos Veracruz. On Food Truck Fridays, there is no reason to stay home and cook. Just show up hungry and with a hankering to the fête that is accompanied by an artisan market of 15 or so vendors and a band in the amphitheater.

1200 Town Center Dr., 561-254-5120
abacoa.com/events

11

POUR SOMETHIN' TALL AND STRONG

AT SQUARE GROUPER TIKI BAR

The neon sign behind the stage, ablaze with the likeness of Jolly Roger, has the words "World Famous" above the notorious logo. Named for the US Coast Guard's code words denoting bales of marijuana thrown from the boats and planes of drug smugglers, Square Grouper Tiki Bar rose to stardom when country-music singer Alan Jackson recorded "It's Five O'Clock Somewhere" on-site with Jimmy Buffett in 2003. Now, killer concerts entertain feverish crowds every day of the week at the age-21-and-older establishment. A full menu (the Paradise Cheeseburger is a top choice among parrotheads) compliments a full bar. If you pucker up to the Pirates Punch, you will be glad you did. The eats are served pickup style, and you can sit at any table for as long as you want without a waiter or a waitress (there are none) asking you to pay off your tab.

1111 Love St., 561-406-6417
squaregrouper.net

12

DO NOT LET THE HOLE-IN-THE-WALL LOCATION FOOL YOU

AT LITTLE MOIR'S FOOD SHACK

The fish-centric kitchen at Little Moir's Food Shack lures diners to suite D3 in an unassuming strip mall near an intersection relentlessly riddled with traffic. They come for fish from all across Florida, the Panhandle to the Keys. They come for fish from the Pacific Rim, the West Coast to South America. They come for fish from the North Atlantic. Most of all, they come for the sweet potato–crusted fish over salad, a dish served the first day the shack did business. The signature offering, along with the fried tuna and basil roll with spicy melon-wasabi dipping sauce, are as popular as ever. The chef-owned restaurant has earned accolades from the *New York Times* and *Southern Living* magazine, received air time on a local PBS television series titled *Check Please! South Florida*, and topped many a list of best places to eat in the region.

103 S US Hwy. 1, Ste. D3, 561-741-3626
littlemoirsjupiter.com/food-shack

TIP

In a tasty twist of fate, the head of Little Moir's Food Shack, Mike Moir, made a comment one day about all the leftover food in the refrigerator while planning the daily handwritten menu. Leftovers Café was born. A sister restaurant to the original, it feeds customers in Abacoa Town Center. In another tasty twist, a third affiliated restaurant called Hibiscus StrEATery opened in the middle of the COVID-19 pandemic, when the building Moir used for catering became dormant. With no parties to plan, he started selling fish from a cooler. Then he added a few tables and chairs and a bit of island décor. It did not take long before word on the "streat" spread.

Leftovers Café
451 University Blvd., 561-627-6030
littlemoirsjupiter.com/leftovers-cafe

Hibiscus StrEATery
326 Hibiscus St., 561-529-3769
littlemoirsjupiter.com/hibiscus-streatery

13

DITCH YOUR DIET
AT JUPITER DONUTS

For out-of-this-world, ring-shaped pieces of sugary dough, land your lips on one of more than 40 highly engineered flavors of fried euphoria at Jupiter Donuts. But first, ground yourself. Once you bite into a Butter Crunch, Cookies ’n Cream, or French Toast creation, your sense of taste is going to launch to infinity and beyond. And second, stop counting calories. The Heath Bar, Maple Bacon, and Red Velvet goodies are to be devoured guilt-free. Third, never mind the cholesterol levels or fat grams. Simply vow to make another trip to the gym after swallowing a Samoa, S’mores, or Snickers variety. Finally, smell the rich chocolate and spicy cinnamon swirling in the atmosphere—fallout from the baking team that reports for duty at midnight. Open at 6 a.m., the galley of gluttony closes at 1 p.m.—or earlier if sales leave its shelves bare.

141 Center St., 561-741-5290
420 US Hwy. 1, North Palm Beach, 561-557-5291
jupiterdonuts.com

SEE FOOD AND EAT IT
AT THE JUPITER SEAFOOD FESTIVAL

Some of the most succulent seafood in all of Florida comes from the crystal-clear waters off Jupiter, making the annual fete that celebrates the belly-pleasing bounty of the ocean a not-to-miss event. The Jupiter Seafood Festival washes ashore in the middle of February at Carlin Park. Vendor tents strewn across the lawn provide plentiful portions of top-notch grub to the public. In addition to fish, the offerings include clams, crab, lobster, mussels, oysters, shrimp, and more. The focus is seafood, but you can munch on chicken, gravitate toward a gyro, or indulge in a slice of pizza if you must. The weekend extravaganza's nautical theme extends beyond delicious delights and into children's happenings, merchandise, and musical performances. The long-running family-friendly festival sometimes sees a plundering pirate or two, so keep an eye out for Blackbeard. Bring your blankets, your chairs, and your appetite.

400 A1A, 561-628-7911
jupiterseafoodfestival.net

15

BELLY UP—LITERALLY—
TO RALPH'S STAND UP BAR

In Palm Beach County's oldest beer-pouring and booze-flowing business, patrons downing drinks at the wooden, waist-high counter do not sit on stools. Rather, they rest a foot on the metal rail that runs along the base of Ralph's Stand Up Bar. Reminiscent of an old Western saloon, minus the spittoons on the floor, the celebrated watering hole glows dimly from a set of pendulous stained-glass pub lights. Instead of tied-off horses, motorcycles line the parking lot out front. There is plenty of whiskey to go around. Formerly called Ralph's Fishing Camp, the storied gin mill originally stood next to a bridge by the Jupiter Inlet Lighthouse. In the early '50s, it moved to Center Street. When there is no band playing, you can shoot discs down the shuffleboard table. A cute outdoor patio in the back enables everyone to breathe in the balmy South Florida weather.

113 Center St., 561-746-6812
ralphsstandupbar.com

BASK IN BOHEMIAN VIBES
AT PERK COFFEE HOUSE

Way more than a java joint, Perk Coffee House brings California dreamin' from sunny Los Angeles to the tiny village of Tequesta via inventive bites, fascinating sips, and mod merchandise. Ever had a chia yogurt bowl? It comes with berries, coconut, and granola. Perk Toast, a sweet take on avocado toast, is topped with peanut butter, banana slices, California Gold Dust, and honey. Plump raisins and pumpkin seeds garnish the wacky watermelon and feta salad. Headlining the drink list are Perk's "Medical Magic" lattes—the collagen latte, the honey-ginger latte, and the Miss Macchiato latte specifically meant for girls. To remain PC, there is a Mr. Macchiato latte just for guys. Bags of Santa Monica Vegobears, packaged organic candy, protein bars and snacks, bottles of flavored fire cider, and trippy jewelry and trinkets can be purchased to go. Come on Sunday mornings for outdoor entertainment.

384 Tequesta Dr., Tequesta, 561-406-5551
perkcoffeehouse.com

CHILL OUT
AT MATTY'S GELATO FACTORY

The swirled scrumptiousness seen behind the glass at Matty's Gelato Factory tantalizes the senses. Colorful tins of the frozen dairy product form a rainbow of flavors as far out as Blood Orange Raspberry Sorbet and OMG Coffee Chocolate Mascarpone. Know ahead of time it will be difficult to choose. "Decisions, decisions," a local newspaper wrote. "Always a tough one when they're all good." The owner whips up the creamy novelties daily, striving to develop recipes that will keep customers coming back for cones and cups. First discovered by a local magazine, the "seriously delicious" Italian ice cream received another rave review in *Travel + Leisure*. The national publication named it the best ice cream shop in the state, "ready to be spooned by the beach," which is a block away. If salted caramel, sugar-free mango, or vegan vanilla suit you, stop in for a scoop.

867 Donald Ross Rd., Juno Beach, 561-557-3539
mattysgelatofactory.com

18

SAY AYE, AYE
AT CAPTAIN CHARLIE'S ORIGINAL REEF GRILL

An aging, faded box sign lights up every evening after five, drawing droves of diners like moths to a flame. Those eager to eat early arrive and wait in ratty old chairs facing the parking lot. Partially blocked from view by a three-story office building, the much-raved-about restaurant's drab exterior easily would be missed by someone not in the know. *Wine Spectator* magazine found it, though, and featured it in an article titled "Hiding In Plain Sight." That was in 2011. Captain Charlie's Original Reef Grill has grown in popularity since then, but the truth is the business has been a rock star for more than 30 years. Ten or more types of fresh fish are available most nights, baked, blackened, broiled, or cooked any way you prefer. Duck and quail are exotically prepared as are a plethora of pastas and other clever concoctions only the mind of a seasoned chef could conjure.

12846 US Hwy. 1, Juno Beach, 561-624-9924
captaincharliesreefgrillfl.com

CLINK AND DRINK
AT THE VINE POST

A quaint, quiet venue for sipping reds, whites, rosés, and more, The Vine Post has a varietal to please everyone's palate. Those looking for cool, comfortable confines to toast a day well-spent will encounter the perfect pour at a bountiful bar. For oenophiles wanting to add to their collection, the well-stocked shop will part with its best bottles. A focus on small production lines almost guarantees you will sample something new while learning about it at the same time. A glass of sparkling goes for as little as $10, or you can take home 750 milliliters of Bordeaux or Burgundy for upward of $1,000. Also, there are three dozen craft beers available for those who prefer hops over grapes. Guests can bring their own food, order from a delivery service, or have plates brought in from one of The Vine Post's partner restaurants.

817 Donald Ross Rd., Juno Beach, 561-935-1720
thevinepost.com

GET SCONED
AT TEAPOTS & TREASURES CAFÉ

The British quick bread that has accompanied the afternoon ritual of the royals for centuries arrives before you on old-fashioned china at Teapots & Treasures Café. Bits of blueberries and cranberries with lemon and orange zest modernize the little restaurant's scones, yet when they are served with a spot of Earl Grey or English Breakfast make you feel like a descendent of the king. The lovable lunch locale presents distinguished cakes, cookies, and other petite desserts, cocoa and coffee, and tea, glorious tea. Raspberry Tipsy Tea spiked with prosecco is the signature drink. For a savory experience, pair a salad, a sandwich, or a bowl of soup with some wine. Instead of ordering *a la carte*, you can take advantage of all-inclusive services named after Queen Elizabeth or Princess Diana. While you sip, browse the boutique, whose courtly gifts are worthy of raising a pinky.

14137 US Hwy. 1, Juno Beach, 561-881-0447
teapotsandtreasurescafe.com

21

WEAR YOUR WET BATHING SUIT
AT CATHY'S BEACH CONNECTION

Kenny Chesney's "No Shoes, No Shirt, No Problems" could qualify as the theme song for Cathy's Beach Connection. The unconventional joint whose rustic outdoor deck fills up rapidly for lunch and dinner embraces beachgoers. An ingenious water-misting system under the big blue awning keeps you cool while you revel in a frothy mug of beer and a crunchy fish sandwich. You do not have to go inside to use the bathroom. Come as you are, kick back on a picnic bench, and be amused by the offbeat décor. If it is a particularly hot day or night, and you need air conditioning, there is an inside seating area with a small bar where you can eat. The room is similarly decorated, and everything hanging on the walls is for sale. Cathy's Beach Connection equally embraces little beachgoers and has several super-inexpensive children's selections.

12850 US Hwy. 1, Juno Beach, 561-626-2262
cathysbeachconnection.com

GRAB A GROWLER TO GO
AT TWISTED TRUNK BREWING

If indeed Benjamin Franklin said, “Beer is proof that God loves us and wants us to be happy,” everyone’s favorite founding father would have loved the totally fun taproom at Twisted Trunk Brewing. A huge bar with clear views of the stainless-steel vessels inside the brewery provides pints for the people. Mainstays for the masses include Gardens Gold, a light lager; IPGA, an India pale ale; and Palm Beach Pilz, a tart pilsner. Specialty brews show up on a rotating basis. Customers can take their favorite flavors home in a logoed growler. Flat-screen TVs entertain those inside, while cornhole games entertain those outside. Twisted Trunk Brewing’s name pays homage to the historic banyan tree at Northlake and MacArthur Boulevards, the official entrance to Palm Beach Gardens. A neon-lit sculptural interpretation of the famed *ficus benghalensis* adorns a wall as do old photos of the city.

2000 PGA Blvd., Palm Beach Gardens, 561-671-2337
twistedtrunkbrewing.com

TIP

The older sibling of Twisted Trunk Brewing, Tequesta Brewing Company has a similar MO. You can take the Prickly Pear Wheat, an easy-to-drink ale that will fill your beer gut, or any other on-tap quencher in a carry-out growler.

287 S US Hwy. 1, Tequesta, 561-745-5000, tequestabrewing.com

SAVOR THE FLAVOR OF KEY WEST, FLORIDA, AT TULIPAN BAKERY & CAFÉ

Café con leches and *media noches* fly out of the Cuban grocery stores and mom-and-pop kitchens found on almost every corner of the Old Town area in the Southernmost City. Those longing for the Latin flavors of the island do not have to wait until their next vacation to taste them. Tulipan Bakery & Café, a yummy shop in North Palm Beach, has an indulgent menu that will make deciding what type of coffee to order and which sandwich you want to sink your teeth into a difficult task. *Buchi* or *cortadito*? Chorizo or steak? The family-owned restaurant also serves an assortment of savory *croquettes*, *empanadas*, and *rellenas*, and sweet, fruit-filled pastries. Its fresh-squeezed orange juice is a big seller as is the *guarapo*. Take a box of *café con leche* and a platter of cakes, cookies, cream puffs, or other decadent desserts with you in a nod to *Cayo Hueso*.

731 Northlake Blvd., North Palm Beach, 561-842-4847
tulipanbakery.com

FESTEGGIARE ALL THINGS ITALIAN AT THE FEAST OF LITTLE ITALY

The co-founders of the annual street fair describe it as an opportunity for festivalgoers from all walks of life to come together as one big *famiglia*. Like warm hugs from loved ones, pasta dishes, pizza pies, and hearty portions of sausage and peppers comfort the body. Like kisses on the cheek, *cannolis*, *sfogliatellas*, and *zeppoles* deliver sweetness to the soul. Like pats on the back from old friends, the sounds of Dean Martin, Frank Sinatra, and Frankie Valli emanating from the entertainment stage act as adoring welcomes. So, if you are in town in early November, hit up the outdoor celebration of food and drink from the land of the green, white, and red flag, and be sure to try the orange Aperol Spritz. The Feast of Little Italy will stir your passions as you experience the culture and heritage of *Italia*.

Abacoa Town Center
1267 Main St., 561-427-0500
feastoflittleitaly.com

25

BE A WISE GUY
AT PLANT BASED MAFIA

A vegan restaurant has gone to the mattresses in Palm Beach Gardens. Led by Danny Costanzo, the founder of Plant Based Mafia, war is being waged against disease, illness, and the immunocompromised. Costanzo's strategy advances the ideals of health and happiness. His tactics amass appetizers, entrées, sides, and sweets. His weaponry targets ingredients instead of enemies. "We Don't Whack Animals, We Whack Plants," his cheeky motto, sums up the mission in Sicilian-ese. Diagnosed with coronary artery failure at age 40, Costanzo, who at one point weighed 375 pounds, had an epiphany. He decided to quit his stressful, six-figure job and embark on a movement to adopt a 100-percent plant-based lifestyle and recapture his wellness. He did, developing a *Godfather*-themed catalog of dishes defiantly dubbed Don't "Breaka" My Balls, Get the "F" Outta Here, Not Your Momma's Meat Sauce, The Big Bambino, and more.

7100 Fairway Dr., Palm Beach Gardens, 561-223-2432
plantbasedmafia.com

TWO ADDITIONAL RESTAURANTS WHOSE FOOD WILL FAKE OUT THE MANLIEST OF MEAT-EATERS

Christopher's Kitchen
Mainstreet at Midtown, 4783 PGA Blvd.
Palm Beach Gardens, 561-318-6191
christopherskitchenfl.com

Mood
235 S US Hwy. 1
Tequesta, 561-766-2317
moodvegan.com

A scene from *Sweet Charity*
at the Maltz Jupiter Theater
Photo courtesy of Jason Nuttle

MUSIC AND ENTERTAINMENT

SOAK UP THE STAGE
AT THE MALTZ JUPITER THEATRE

The award-winning regional performing-arts center has humble roots. Hometown hero Burt Reynolds, who wanted to bring culture to an area that, at the time, had none, envisioned a stage for a segment of society never exposed to the dramatic arts. Reynolds's dream started with a mound of dirt on the side of an unpaved road east of US Highway 1. It became reality after he brought acting buddies Dom DeLuise and Charles Nelson Reilly to town to show them the location. The Burt Reynolds Dinner Theatre broke ground in 1978 and debuted in 1979. Known as the "Miracle at the Truck Stop," a phrase Reilly coined, its glitzy run ended in 1996. In 2001, a nonprofit formed to take ownership of the famed building. Renovated as the Maltz Jupiter Theatre, it has undergone several major expansions and now produces pre-Broadway musicals beneath a dazzling proscenium arch.

1001 E Indiantown Rd., 561-575-2223
jupitertheatre.org

TIP

Prior to enjoying a production at the largest facility of its kind in Florida, take a moment to visit a raucous remnant of the Burt Reynolds Dinner Theatre. Sculpted by Cuban artist Manuel Carbonell, the life-size statue depicts the Bandit bare-chested and barefoot on a bucking horse. The piece stood in front of the main doors until 1989. A town grant paid for its restoration and installment at the corner of Indiantown Road and A1A.

WELCOME THE HOLIDAYS IN SOUTH FLORIDA STYLE

AT THE PALM BEACH HOLIDAY BOAT PARADE

The Marine Industries Association of Palm Beach County ushers in the most wonderful time of the year by staging the Palm Beach Holiday Boat Parade. A twinkling procession of well-decked-out watercraft, it almost always occurs in three-quarter-length-sleeve weather. The eight-mile route on the Intracoastal Waterway begins in North Palm Beach, led by a fireworks-shooting barge, and ends at the Jupiter Inlet Lighthouse. Plenty of public viewing sites are available along the way. Watching the lighted vessels glide through the night—ornaments swaying from the halyards, Santa Clauses waving from the tuna towers, elves dancing to music carried by the wind—you know you are in the Sunshine State. The event benefits the US Marine Corps Reserve Toys for Tots Foundation, and you can contribute by waving a flashlight at one of the "toy fleet" boats and donating an unwrapped gift to the uniformed officer onboard.

561-863-0012
marinepbc.org/boat-parade

HEAR LIVE, LOCAL MUSIC
AT MAXI'S LINEUP

The three-dozen-seat venue is the place to be while you wait for your table—and there more than likely will be a wait—at Little Moir's Food Shack. The owner of the restaurant that belies its hole-in-the-wall location opened the adjoining space to quell the loss of customers who would take one look at the long line of patrons waiting to get in the door and bail. It worked—almost too well. With a roster of working musicians from the surrounding community, Maxi's Lineup has become as much of a destination as Little Moir's Food Shack. Guests can order from a creative menu complete with a one-of-a-kind "Drink of the Night," crafty "Shackatizers," and "Worldly Plates," and, for dessert, homemade ice cream and other sweets. Be warned; its cozy, enjoyable, listening-room-like atmosphere might make you forget about that wait for your table next door.

103 S US Hwy. 1, Ste. D3, 561-741-3626
littlemoirsjupiter.com/maxis-lineup

TIP

The live, local music scene in Palm Beach County is amped. Bands bang out the blues and crank out the country all over town. Whether you prefer reggae or rock 'n' roll, you have landed in the right arena. Here are a few key locales to catch some tunes.

Uncle Eddie's Ristorante
Authentic Old Country fare dished out with hefty portions of piano playing, sing-alongs, and Andrea Bocelli tributes
4050 S US Hwy. 1, 561-508-7799
uncleeddiesristorante.com

Uncle Mick's Bar & Grill
Different bands each week plus darts, poker, pool, karaoke, and line dancing
6671 W Indiantown Rd., Ste. 61, 561-743-8330
unclemicks.com

Nick & Johnny's Osteria
Themed shows in the dining room and casual listening in the lounge accentuated by flavors from the Italian kitchen
14133 US Hwy. 1, Juno Beach, 561-318-5466
nickandjohnnysosteria.com

Thirsty Turtle Seagrill
A slick seafood joint that rocks on the weekends
13981 US Hwy. 1, Juno Beach, 561-627-8991
thirstyturtlefl.com/juno-beach

HOP ATOP
A FLOATING TIKI BAR

Take your happy hour up a notch and spend it on a decorative vessel stocked with adult beverages that cruises pleasurably along the Intracoastal Waterway. *Mahalo* as the party of a pontoon boat is called has a bunch of options for heading out on the water in the early evenings. It also charters private runs to ring in special occasions—birthdays, reunions, weddings, and more. Part of the PonTiki fleet, the 65-passenger vessel sets sail from its slip at Harbourside Place near the orange kiosk. Reservations are required as is the completion of a safety waiver, both of which can be taken care of online. Prices include beer, wine, hard seltzers, bottled water, and ice, music, and a guided tour of the area by the captain and first mate. For families with children, a morning cruise to one of the local sandbars is a best bet.

200 N US Hwy. 1, 833-766-8454
pontiki.com

SETTLE IN FOR DINNER AND A MOVIE AT CINÉPOLIS

Recline in luxurious leather seats, put your feet up like you would if you were home, and make the most of a motion picture at Cinépolis. While you watch the latest blockbuster on the big screen, order a lobster grilled cheese sandwich from the menu and a California chardonnay from the bar with the touch of a button. A waiter or waitress will arrive with your refreshments. Still hungry? Bottomless bowls of popcorn and shareable servings of candy are great for snacking in the dark. As the film enters the third act, do not forget about dessert. On Tuesdays, tickets are half-price. During the week, select titles can be seen for $5 compliments of the Cinépolis Handpicked programming series. The theater also has daily deals—discounted tickets for children and seniors on some days and $5 Bloody Marys and $10 tequila sunrises on others.

201 N US Hwy. 1, 561-277-1740
cinepolisusa.com

TIP

If you decide to save your appetite for a meal post-flick, Del Pesto is in the same shopping center. The Italian restaurant has all the hearty tastes covered and also makes pies in its New York–style pizzeria that specializes in Neapolitan crusts.

561-768-9533, delpestojupiter.com

TEST YOUR LUCK
AT THE JUPITER IRISH FEST

The St. Patrick's Day affair brings the best of the Emerald Isle to town every March. Kilt-wearing members of the Palm Beach County Professional Firefighters Pipes & Drums fill the air with the strains of tradition. Steppers from the Florida-based Tir Na Greine School of Irish Dance perform sprightly routines. Sportsmen from the Orlando Gaelic Athletic Association challenge one another, and any daring member of the public, in the 3,000-year-old heritage of hurling, the fastest game on grass. For the $5 price of admission, you will feel as if the wind at your back propelled you across the pond. For an extra $25—the cost to sample a flight of whiskey—you will be blessed with three shots and a commemorative T-shirt. Round-the-clock music, costume contests for children and adults, and a pull-your-own-pint workshop will give you plenty of opportunities to have some *craic*.

Abacoa Town Center
1267 Main St., 561-262-7087
jupiteririshfest.com

TIP

When the calendar turns the page to April, and the corned beef and cabbage, the Guinness, and the Jameson are mere memories, the time has come to *laissez les bons temps rouler* at the Cajun Crawfish & Music Festival, also at Abacoa Town Center. Fast forward to July, and the patriotic Mega Bash brings two days of baseball to Roger Dean Chevrolet Stadium, capped by a fireworks extravaganza.

Cajun Crawfish & Music Festival
561-427-0500
cajuncrawfishmusicfestival.com

Mega Bash
4751 Main St., 561-775-1818
rogerdeanchevroletstadium.com

APPRECIATE THE ACOUSTICS
OF AN AXMAN

Geoff Livingston has plucked the bass and strummed the six-string in South Florida since moving here in 1984. A town resident, Livingston belongs to a pair of well-put-together bands, The Powercats and The Shareholders, both known for their blues and classic rock covers. When not jamming with his mates up and down the Palm Beach County coast, he performs acoustic solo sets of '50s, '60s, and '70s favorites with a few pop numbers in the mix. He can knock out almost any tune and gladly takes requests. If you attend a show, expect to hear hits from America, Bread, and Jimmy Buffett, plus his specialties—Nancy Sinatra's "These Boots Are Made for Walkin'," Bruce Channel's "Hey! Baby," and Pure Prairie League's "Amie." His haunts include Ralph's Stand Up Bar, Blue Pointe Bar and Grill, and Angelo's Italian Restaurant's Toney Penna Drive location.

561-818-7026
facebook.com/geofflivingstonacousticandvocals

33

UNLEASH YOUR INNER PICASSO

AT UPTOWN PAINT AND SIP

Seeing your canvas come to life with every brush stroke while savoring something alcoholic for creativity's sake is a shoe-in for the *100 Things* list. Uptown Paint and Sip has weekly classes open to students with artistic aspirations as well as to students who never have picked up a palette. Professional instructors lead the group, step by step, through the processes and techniques of applying color to achieve the desired scene, whether it is a pelican perched on a piling, a hammock drooping between a pair of palm trees, or a sailboat silhouetted against the horizon. After the two-hour-or-so session, the painting is yours to take home. If you want to unleash your inner Pollack instead of your inner Picasso, book the Splatter Room. Inside, you can fling fluorescent paint in the obscurity of black lights to the pulse of disco music.

1695 W Indiantown Rd., Ste. 12, 561-295-5255
uptownpaintandsip.com

ROLLICK IN THE ROLL-IN

AT THE SOUTH EAST CLASSICS MONTHLY CAR SHOW

Engines rumble. Chrome shines. Heads turn. The South East Classics Monthly Car Show's bad-to-the-bone automobiles in all their vintage glory definitely dress up the streets of Harbourside Place. Vehicles belonging to members of the nonprofit club date back at least 25 years. Among the super-fine rides that might catch your eye are Barracudas, Bel Airs, Camaros, Chargers, Chevelles, Corvettes, Cougars, Falcons, GTOs, Impalas, Mustangs, Novas, and really old pickups. At one of the events, a 1909 Sears buggy dominated the day. A 1950 Willys wagon did the same at another. Attending all or part of the four-hour affair will leave you hungry for a hotrod. The presentation of Spectators Choice and Participants Choice awards wraps up the rally. South East Classics additionally converges monthly on Angelo's Italian Restaurant's Toney Penna Drive location for a show complemented by a good band and even better pizza.

200 N US Hwy. 1 and 155 Toney Penna Dr., 772-216-9488
southeastclassics.org

35

LOUNGE AND LISTEN
AT BLUE POINTE BAR AND GRILL

A drinking establishment with a swimming hole is a grand idea, and Blue Pointe Bar and Grill on the Intracoastal Waterway has a spectacular sip, splish, and splash setup. Usually reserved for luxury cruise ships and resort hotels, pool bars have a way of making you feel like a boss kicking back at your own over-the-top oasis. The fact that one exists in the area—and that the public can crash it—is reason enough to visit. Not only are the food (try the signature lobster flatbread with brie and mozzarella) and drinks (choose one of a handful of rum concoctions overflowing from a bucket) to be enjoyed, so is the entertainment. The schedule runs seven days a week and has multiple artists booked every Friday, Saturday, and Sunday afternoon. If your skin starts to prune, hit the deck in a comfortable Adirondack chair.

18701 US Hwy. 1, Tequesta, 561-406-6270
bluepointebarandgrill.com

TIP

Tiki 52 Bar & Grille, the neighbor to the north of Blue Point Bar and Grill, also has live music. It flows from the open-air eatery and tropical hut dripping with Caribbean soul.

18487 US Hwy. 1, Tequesta, 561-746-3312, blowingrocksmarina.com

WAVE YOUR LIGHTER
AT CARLIN PARK AFTER DARK

The entertainment series that highlights tribute bands throws it back to when you had to camp out at the record store to get concert tickets, when stadium beers cost a lot less than they do now, and when smartphones were not even a glimmer in Apple's eye. Carlin Park After Dark's free shows pay homage to the great bands and favorite genres of the music industry. Each act's replicative wardrobe, spot-on stage presence, and familiar sound will have you believing it is 1985 all over again. Previous performances featured Chain Reaction (a Journey tribute), Jaded (an Aerosmith tribute), Simply Tina (a Tina Turner tribute), and Solid Brass (a Chicago tribute). Every seat is on the lawn, so bring a blanket or a chair. You can pack drinks and snacks and pre-game in the parking lot in the hour leading up to showtime.

Seabreeze Amphitheatre
750 S A1A, 561-966-7043
pbcparks.com

TIP

The wailing guitars, booming kickdrums, and loud voices of more tribute bands can be heard at the monthly Live Concert Series at Abacoa Amphitheater. Also at the Abacoa Amphitheater, jazz, brunch, and Bloodys fill the bill on select Sundays. On select Saturdays at Downtown Palm Beach Gardens, you can see solos, duos, and trios play at the interactive water fountain. Here are the details.

Live Concert Series at Abacoa Amphitheater/
Live Jazz Series at Abacoa Amphitheater
1260 University Blvd., 561-469-6700
abacoa.com/events

Sounds at Downtown
11701 Lake Victoria Gardens Ave.
Palm Beach Gardens, 561-727-2640
downtownpbg.com/events

GATHER 'ROUND THE TABLE
AT TAYLOR FARMHOUSE CAFÉ AND CATERING

The rurally rooted restaurant serves supper and song every evening in its happy homestead west of town. Taylor Farmhouse Café and Catering feeds families and friends gathered for good-ole American eats prepared by an experienced husband-and-wife team whose love of food knows no bounds. Banjos, fiddles, and guitars nourish neighbors with music almost as much as appetizers and entrées nourish bodies with sustenance. Bands bring the nestled-in-pine-needles stage to life with bluegrass, country, and indie rock. Guests snap their fingers and stomp their feet in between bites of alligator fritters with cocktail sauce, Blue Ribbon meatloaf in Merlot demi-glace, and pan-seared whiskey chicken. The tunes can be taken in on the porch, under the shed, and by the bonfire. The casual charm and relaxing aura of the café are apparent at the front door where welcoming words written on a blackboard greet you.

16891 Jupiter Farms Rd., 561-747-8221
jupiterfarmhousecafe.com

38

SPIN THE VINYL AND MORE
AT ANALOGOPOLIS

"Something About You" by Boston blares from the turntable while customers claw through bins and bop their heads to the blast-from-the-past song. Such is a day in the life of Analogopolis, a retro record store that sells artwork-adorned albums with amazing sound made possible by an ultrasonic cleaning process ridding them of dusty-needle noise. Do you yearn for the Norwegian synth of A-ha, the heavy metal of Black Sabbath, or the punk rock of the Sex Pistols? You more than likely will find it among the stacks. If not, the owner more than likely will know how to get it. In addition to music, the inventory encompasses vintage Atari 2600 game cartridges that go way beyond Pong, antique-by-today's-standards tech (think Packard Bell), and posters that will make some of you feel like teenagers again. The hours of operation vary; call first to make sure the "city" is open.

829 Donald Ross Rd., Juno Beach, 561-622-6688
analogopolis.com

PAINT A PIECE OF POTTERY
AT CRAFT HAUS

Great for young ones, the spacious studio open seven days a week invites the public to pull a dish, mug, plaque, vase, or other decorative object off the shelf and get busy with it. At-the-ready staff members love working with children and are on hand to give instructions and tips and teach tricks of the trade. Whether choosing individual colors to cover your creation or opting for one of the silkscreen selections, everyone will go home happy. Craft Haus also can glaze and fire the artwork for you with pickup a week later. Several classes, like Mommy & Me, take place throughout the week if you and your family want to plan an outing ahead of time. Feel like testing your skills and taking the making process up a notch? Set up a lesson at Clay Haus a few doors down and try your hand at wheel throwing.

11701 Lake Victoria Gardens Ave., Palm Beach Gardens
Craft Haus: Ste. 4102, 561-630-3450
Clay Haus: Ste. 7102, 561-355-5906
clayhauspalmbeach.com

40

CATCH A SHOW
BY A PRO

David Goodman's unmistakable voice, superior songwriting skills, and passion for playing make the nationally known, locally based musician a must-see. From Los Angeles to Nashville with a salty stint in Key West, Florida, along the way, Goodman has gigged on stages big and small and in front of adoring audiences of all ages for nearly five decades. He now calls Palm Beach Gardens home. You can find him pickin' and a-grinnin' at bars and restaurants throughout the area. The crowds might get a little lively at the bars and a tad talkative at the restaurants, but no matter the venue, the man behind the mic emerges as much more than background noise. He sings about it in an original titled "This Guitar": "Now most of you will drink your beer / Never even know that I was here / A few of you will draw in near / In hopes that I will stay."

561-758-6064
davidgoodmanonline.com

A juvenile green sea turtle rehabs at the Loggerhead Marinelife Center. Photo courtesy of Sarah Edwards

SPORTS AND RECREATION

ROOT, ROOT, ROOT FOR THE HOME TEAMS

AT ROGER DEAN CHEVROLET STADIUM

The Miami Marlins and the St. Louis Cardinals report to Roger Dean Chevrolet Stadium every February for Spring Training. Every March, fans flock to the sunny sports arena for one of the most-hailed happenings of the year. Locals start counting their sick days at work as soon as the schedule is announced. Likewise, visitors from the Magic City and the Gateway City plan their pilgrimages. The "fish" and the "redbirds" draw fierce followings, for sure, but other teams from the Grapefruit League cross the state for matchups that take the hype to the next level. Two of them are the Boston Red Sox and the New York Yankees. The Houston Astros and the Washington Nationals, whose Spring Training headquarters is in West Palm Beach, play in Jupiter, too. At a preseason Major League Baseball game, you never know what—or whom—you are going to see.

4751 Main St., 561-775-1818
rogerdeanchevroletstadium.com

MEET THE CAST OF CHARACTERS

AT BUSCH WILDLIFE SANCTUARY

Arvy the brown pelican, Gary the Canada goose, and Stu the whistling duck; river otters Charlie and Tater Tot; and Greyson the gray fox and Trixie the red fox all belong to a gang of 200 other winged, pawed, and clawed "ambassadors" at Busch Wildlife Sanctuary, a heartwarming haven that relies on donations to keep its rescued animals happy and healthy. Alligators and crocodiles stay cool in the wetland habitat. Giant tortoises take shelter in their dugouts. Black bears wobble through the pines, and Florida panthers pace in their pens. During your visit, you will get up close and personal with beautiful bald eagles, talkative parrots, and wise old owls. If you like snakes, do not miss the serpentarium. The 19-acre property has a 6,880-square-foot environmental education building, a 4,000-square-foot hospital, and a 2,800-square-foot amphitheater. Before you leave, buy something adorable in the gift shop.

17855 Rocky Pines Rd., 561-575-3399
buschwildlife.org

WET A LINE

Capt. Marvin Steiding promises a day of action-packed fishing aboard *Sea Candy*, a Prowler Express that runs both offshore charters in search of big game and inshore trips for a more laid-back experience. The waters in and around the Jupiter area teem with tuna and other species such as dolphin, kingfish, and wahoo. If you are lucky enough to hook a marlin or a sailfish, the fight will invigorate you and give you a tall tale to tell for years to come. All edible fish you catch can be kept if you choose, and *Sea Candy*'s crew handily fillets and bags it for you. The large guys, namely marlin and sailfish, will be released, but not before you are photographed with your creature. Outings range from as short as three hours to as long as eight hours, and Capt. Marvin also takes groups to the Bahamas.

1075 N A1A, 561-666-8266
seacandyfishing.com

TIP

With many a world record in the recreational fishing industry set locally, it comes as no surprise that the charter business abounds in a multitude of marinas near the Jupiter Inlet. Here are some other outfits.

Adrenaline Rush Charters
Capt. Tim Mackay
1095 N A1A, 561-427-4913
arushcharters.com

Native Guide Fishing Charters
Capt. Charlie Stuve
1095 N A1A, 561-262-2652
nativeguidejupiter.com

Black Dog
Capt. Bill Taylor
1111 Love St., 561-744-5700
blackdogfishing.com

Country Club Drift Fishing
Capt. Jim Barton
1111 Love St., 561-262-5329
countryclubcharters.com

Good Time Charter Fishing
Capt. Byron Allen
1111 Love St., 561-277-5941
goodtimecharterfishing.com

Latitude Sportfishing
Capt. Larry McCarthy
1111 Love St., 561-537-0553
latitudesportfishing.com

Mystic Rose Fishing Charters
Capt. Jay York
1111 Love St., 561-371-1172
mysticrosefishingcharters.com

Red Beard Fishing Charters
Capt. Howard Tuttle
1111 Love St., 561-644-7668
facebook.com/redbeardfishing

PLAY PUTT-PUTT
AT LIGHTHOUSE COVE ADVENTURE GOLF

With two sportive locations from which to choose, Lighthouse Cove Adventure Golf will challenge and charm those who have set their sights on sinking putts. The one near the beach has double the fun with a pair of courses, Lost Lagoon and Paradise Falls. Lost Lagoon takes golfers through caves and hilly terrain and also passes by an impressive aquarium housing all kinds of tropical fish. Paradise Falls is dotted with cute and colorful props such as floating boats and leaping dolphins placed amid the water features. Abacoa Town Center's Lighthouse Cove Adventure Golf bears a slight degree of difficulty as its tricky turf creates a game of risk vs. reward. If you birdie (or bogie), why not celebrate (or commiserate) with a beer? Call to place your order, and a staff member will deliver your drinks directly to your hole.

617 N A1A, 561-203-7965
lighthousecoveminigolf.com/jupiter
1145 Main St., 561-268-2717
lighthousecoveminigolf.com/abacoa

TIP

If putt-putt leaves you longing for a real 18-hole experience, tee off at Sandhill Crane Golf Club. The 72-par course set within the Loxahatchee Slough, where sightings of the tall and stately birds are common, welcomes players of all skills. A public facility with reasonable rates, its 19th hole is The Dancing Crane restaurant. Toast your score in air-conditioned comfort with some well-deserved refreshments.

9500 Sandhill Crane Dr., Palm Beach Gardens
561-630-1160, pbgfl.com

KAYAK
TO AN ISLAND

Paddling Jupiter's blueways beneath sunny skies can lead you to several spectacular spots depending on the time and effort you want to put into your adventure. From one of a plethora of put-ins, you can explore the Loxahatchee River's "Wild and Scenic" Southwest Fork, the Northwest Fork that hugs a shoreline rimmed with gorgeous homes, or the North Fork that flows into the Intracoastal Waterway. Sawfish Bay Park, on the North Fork, has a large launch area close to Sawfish Island, a nine-acre mass of trees and swamps. After the short jaunt, you can get out of your boat, pull it onto a small patch of sand, and walk through the scrub. Be sure to wear your hydra shoes. If you feel like channeling Magellan, climb back in the cockpit and circumnavigate the key. In favorable conditions, it will take you no more than one hour.

1133 Alt. A1A, 561-741-2400
jupiter.fl.us/facilities

TIP

When you return to Sawfish Bay Park, check out the Florida East Coast Railway Jupiter Train Depot, a 100-plus-year-old relic painted bright yellow. The restored building in the south part of the park saw many a choo-choo chug through town during the height of Henry Flagler's track-laying enterprise. Of the more than two dozen depots originally built along the railroad that ran from Jacksonville to the Keys, the Jupiter station is one of fewer than 10 left standing.

SOOTHE THE SENSES AND THE SOUL
AT JUPITER BEACH RESORT & SPA

The seaside hotel dripping in tropical décor has a suite of private rooms where you can treat yourself to a facial, a massage, or some other beneficial body treatment. As you enter Jupiter Beach Resort & Spa's sanctuary, sounds of water fill your ears. Blue and green hues bring the ocean indoors. Ameliorating aromas move you into a meditative state. After checking in, the relaxation lounge awaits. There, guests can listen to stress-relieving resonance and inhale ultra-therapeutic scents while preparing for their services, all of which are performed on vibracoustic tables. Following your session, imbibe an adaptogen from the elixir bar and head to the social lounge, an outdoor space shaded by palm trees with a view of the beach. The biophilic design of the Jupiter Beach Resort & Spa allows everyone to improve upon his or her overall well-being through *salus per aquam*.

5 N A1A, 561-746-2511
opalcollection.com/jupiter-beach

TIP

PGA National Resort's spa will have you breathing deeply as soon as you encounter the 40,000-square-foot, 29-room mecca of mindfulness. The calming colors that paint the space, a mix of champagne shades and coral blushes, will relax you almost as much as your esthetician. The *pièce de résistance* is the immaculate outdoor deck and its three therapeutic mineral pools enriched with imported salts from around the world.

400 Avenue of the Champions, Palm Beach Gardens
561-627-3111, pgaresort.com/spa

SNORKEL
CATO'S BRIDGE

The blue-green water beneath the span that connects Jupiter with Jupiter Island reaches depths of 20 feet. Large rocks bed down on the sandy bottom, providing plenty of hiding places for critters. Whether low, slack, or high tide, the exceptional visibility of the local swimming hole makes it a sweet spot for snorkeling. Cato's Bridge traverses the Intracoastal Waterway near the confluence of the Loxahatchee River and the Jupiter Inlet where fresh water, brackish water, and saltwater mingle, attracting a biodiversity of marine life. Don your gear, including fins, to help negotiate the sometimes-strong current, and prepare to encounter angel fish, hog snapper, spiny lobster, stone crab, and other tropical species. Park at the Jupiter Inlet Lighthouse and head north to Beach Road to access the area by foot. Boaters usually tie off at the wooded slope south of the bridge and jump overboard for adventure.

facebook.com/pages/catos-bridge/144703792264701

HIT THE BULLSEYE

AT GAME OF AXES

Have you partaken in the extreme indoor activity known as axe throwing? If so, great! That means you can put your primal skills to use at Game of Axes by grabbing a sharpened weapon and taking aim, maybe even grunting a little and unbosoming the much-memed "Florida Man" that exists somewhere within you. The rustic facility serves beer, wine, and, of course, mead, one of the oldest alcoholic beverages on the planet that pairs thematically with one of the oldest tools on the planet. On select dates, "Glow & Throw" promotions take place from 5 p.m. until closing time, giving you a chance to chuck those babies in the dark. Bring your own food to enjoy or order delivery to add to the party-like atmosphere. And the more the merrier—Game of Axes can accommodate up to 12 guests per lane. Smaller groups are welcome, too.

10160 W Indiantown Rd., 561-228-1228
gameofaxes.com

TIP

Another Game of Axes facility is hacking its way into the city limits of Palm Beach Gardens at 7700 Military Trail, providing yet another place for the emergence of everyone's "Florida Man."

49

GO ON

THE J-TOWN JOYRIDE

The J-town Joyride takes bicycle enthusiasts (who like to drink) on a scenic tour through the prettiest parts of town with stops at two of the most-talked-about libation stations. Led by a local gearhead who grew up in Jupiter, the cruising caper begins at Real Deal Bikes where participants meet up and set out on a sublime six-mile pedal. You will encounter pristine parks, breezy beaches, and the dynamic inlet, pitstopping at the Dive Bar Restaurant and Square Grouper Tiki Bar in between. You can BYOB, too. The J-town Joyride occurs monthly (usually Sunday afternoons but occasionally Saturday nights), and if you miss it, you can rent your own rig on your own time. Why not see the sights like a native and feel the wind in your hair and the sun on your face? It beats any view from behind a windshield.

103 S US Hwy. 1, Ste. E2, 561-746-0585
realdealbikes.com

REAP NATURE'S REWARDS
AT RIVERBEND PARK

Five miles of runs for paddlers. Fifteen miles of trails for hikers and horseback riders as well as bicyclists. Nearly 700 acres of ancient habitat for explorers. Riverbend Park is the *crème de la crème* of Palm Beach County's park system. If traveling by boat, look for alligators sunning themselves on the banks and sliders lined up on logs. Observe herons on the hunt and, if you are fortunate, an eagle soaring overhead. River otters sometimes scramble ashore before slipping back to safety. On *terra firma*, armadillos scavenge, owls burrow, and bobcats and foxes bound through the forest. Riverbend Park, adjacent to Loxahatchee River Battlefield Park, has historical elements, too. The restored farmstead features old tools, a sawmill, and a sugarcane press so you can learn what it was like to live off the land. Pack a picnic for a break beneath a pavilion.

9060 W Indiantown Rd., 561-741-1359
pbcgov.com/parks

STRIKE A POSE

Do a downward-facing dog, come into your strongest warrior pose, and let yourself go during final relaxation—on the sand. Beach yoga beckons the bendable to morning classes on the weekends. Even if you do not consider yourself particularly flexible, give it a try as most of the movements are for beginners. On Saturdays, a class by The Barefoot Yoga Studio takes place one block north of the Juno Beach Pier. Bring your bathing suit or wear it under your clothes so you can wade in afterward for a refreshing dip. The donation-based session ($10 to $20 is suggested) welcomes children to join in the flow for free. On Sundays, Kula Yoga Shala has a class a little farther north near the Jupiter Reef Club that focuses on appreciating the bountiful gifts of nature and recognizing the mind-body connection at the wondrous water's edge.

The Barefoot Yoga Studio
4050 US Hwy. 1, 561-691-4049
thebarefootyogastudio.com

Kula Yoga Shala
400 Toney Penna Dr., 561-339-9642
kulayogashala.com

TIP

Take advantage of two more out-of-the-studio yoga adventures: dock yoga and goat yoga. Dock yoga commences twice a week at Blueline Surf & Paddle Co. where yogis gather before they walk across the street to a semi-sacred space fronting the Loxahatchee River. Goat yoga at Groovy Goat Farm lets lovable little goats jump, literally, into the mix as they playfully plop atop your back.

561-972-6514, breathesaltyoga.com

SPORT YOUR SPOOKIEST COSTUME

AT THE WITCHES & WARLOCKS PADDLE

Nothing screams Halloween in South Florida quite like a witch or a warlock wobbling on the surface, gracelessly gliding downriver on a standup paddleboard. So, if you are in the area come October, save the date for the annual Witches & Warlocks Paddle, a signature event of the Chasin A Dream Foundation. The eerie evening begins with a launch party at Burt Reynolds Park where ghoulish guests gear up for the flotilla. Afterward, the tricks and treats resume at Guanabanas. You can bring your own SUP or rent one from Blueline Surf & Paddle Co. The event is a "friendraiser" for the foundation, whose mission is to assist families in hardship as a result of their children facing cancer or other life-threatening illnesses. Those who would like to contribute to the cause can bring gift cards for gas stations or grocery stores to help with household expenses.

805 US Hwy. 1, 561-315-7005
chasinadream.org

53

MARVEL AT THE MOTION OF THE OCEAN AT BLOWING ROCKS PRESERVE

The natural phenomenon that occurs within Blowing Rocks Preserve, a 73-acre sanctuary on a barrier island, will wow you. At any given moment, a geyser of frothy wet stuff will shoot skyward, traveling up to 50 feet in the air before splashing down on the dramatically shaped Anastasia limestone outcropping. For centuries, the water and the wind have carved the sedimentary rock, forming gaps, holes, and tunnels through which Atlantic rollers are caught and redirected. The action resembles that of hot lava spewing from an erupting volcano. Stunning and surreal, Blowing Rocks Preserve is best visited during high tide with moderate to rough conditions. Bring your cellphone to capture the exhilarating events in photos or on videos. Managed by The Nature Conservancy, the site is open daily with free parking and also features several trails that crisscross the area and a boardwalk that rambles through a mangrove forest.

574 Beach Rd., Tequesta, 561-744-6668
nature.org

TRACK TURTLES
AT LOGGERHEAD MARINELIFE CENTER

One of the most magical things to do on a summer night in South Florida is take a turtle walk. Loggerhead Marinelife Center makes it happen. The center, a nonprofit focused on the research, rehabilitation, care, and conservation of sea turtles, organizes guided tours in June and July, the height of nesting season. Visitors meet at the facility for an educational program on the plight of the species while licensed scouts patrol the beach for females laying eggs. If one is found, the group quietly is led to the site to witness an astounding act of nature. Loggerhead Marinelife Center has several other programs promoting marine conservation, exhibit rooms crammed with interpretive displays, giant aquariums that recreate underwater scenes, and an interactive digital reef. The flippered friends swimming in the 26 outdoor tanks as they heal from illnesses and injuries remain the No. 1 attraction.

14200 US Hwy. 1, Juno Beach, 561-627-8280
marinelife.org

55

EXPERIENCE A SUNRISE
AT THE JUNO BEACH PIER

Gazing upon the horizon as the big orange orb reveals itself, ascending inch by inch out of the ocean, is one of the most gratifying ways to start the morning. Cherish it because not everyone has the opportunity to experience the dawn of a new day as it is meant to be observed. The strand near the Juno Beach Pier presents a picture-perfect place to put your toes in the sand as dark turns to light. Smile and say hello to *el sol*. Then, put on your sunglasses, head up the stairs, and pay the $2 admission fee to walk the length of the 990-foot structure that affords views as far as the eye can see. Catch a glimpse of what the early-to-awake anglers are baiting and hooking. Crack up at the mischievous pelicans hungry for handouts. Clap at the wet-suited surfers shooting the tube.

14775 US Hwy. 1, Juno Beach, 561-855-6185
marinelife.org

56

TROMP THROUGH THE SWAMP
AT THE LOXAHATCHEE SLOUGH

At almost 13,000 acres, the Loxahatchee Slough tops the list as the largest of the nearly three dozen Natural Area sites in Palm Beach County. It also tops the list as the most environmentally diverse. Late summer and early fall, the height of the rainy season, leave the preserve mucky and soggy—the ideal setting for a tromp through the swamp. Wear close-toed shoes, specifically ones that will not slip off your feet as you sink ankle deep into the mud. Also bring a walking stick, not for endurance but for balance. And definitely slather on the sunscreen. Your hike will include flatwoods, hammocks, marshes, prairies, and, of course, swamps. If you do not want to get down and dirty, stay on the multiuse trails lining the perimeter of the park where you will be able to admire the raw beauty of the ecosystem.

11855 Beeline Hwy., Palm Beach Gardens, 561-233-2400
discover.pbcgov.org/erm/naturalareas

TIP

Of the nearly three dozen Natural Area sites in Palm Beach County, six are in Jupiter, one is in Juno Beach, and two are in Palm Beach Gardens.

North Jupiter Flatwoods Natural Area
3377 Church St.

Cypress Creek Natural Area
North parking lot: 10035 Indiantown Rd.
South parking lot: 9424 Indiantown Rd.

Limestone Creek Natural Area
6570 Church St.

Delaware Scrub Natural Area
47 Delaware Blvd.

Pine Glades Natural Area
14122 Indiantown Rd.

Jupiter Ridge Natural Area
1800 US Hwy. 1

Juno Dunes Natural Area
East tract: 14200 US Hwy. 1, Juno Beach
West tract: 14501 US Hwy. 1, Juno Beach

Frenchman's Forest Natural Area
12201 Prosperity Farms Rd., Palm Beach Gardens

Sweetbay Natural Area
12560 Aviation Rd., Palm Beach Gardens

RUSH THE ROPES
AT THE HONDA CLASSIC

With big names, bigger attendance, and even bigger payouts, The Honda Classic is one of the most dynamic and successful sporting events South Florida has ever seen. The competition is intense with commitments from top players on the PGA Tour who battle for the crystal cup on the treacherous Champion Course. Designed by the legendary Jack Nicklaus, a North Palm Beach resident, the course has become famous for three harrowing holes; the 15th, 16th, and 17th collectively are called The Bear Trap. The nationally televised tournament is preceded by a week's worth of fan-friendly activities, celebrations, children's and women's events, kickoff parties, and a pro-am. During each of the four rounds, ticketholders can follow their favorites from tee to green, get up close to the Rickie Fowlers and Rory McIlroys of the world (both are previous winners), and engage with the good-natured gallery.

PGA National Resort
400 Avenue of the Champions, Palm Beach Gardens, 561-799-2747
thehondaclassic.com

FOLLOW
THE JUPITER RIVERWALK

The boater's playground known as the Intracoastal Waterway is accessible to those without boats. A two-and-a-half-mile recreational corridor secures public access to the sparkling thoroughfare from the Jupiter Ridge Natural Area at the south end to the Jupiter Inlet at the north end. Several points of interest can be enjoyed along the way. The redbrick road passes by Mangrove Bay, a community named after—and overlooking—the protected plants whose arched roots harbor fish and other aquatic animals. Also of note is the Lagoon Bridge that takes you across a pond behind the Jupiter Yacht Club, a stretch of nature that would be off-limits to pedestrians and bicyclists if not for the town's master-planned project. The Jupiter Riverwalk continues, hugging Harbourside Place and passing by Burt Reynolds Park. The journey is complete when the Jupiter Inlet Lighthouse towers in the backdrop.

jupiter.fl.us/riverwalk

EXPLORE THE "REAL FLORIDA"

AT JOHN D. MACARTHUR BEACH STATE PARK

The only state park in Palm Beach County preserves for the public a coastal habitat whose environmental importance could have been lost to development. As soon as you turn onto the winding road that leads to the ranger station, you are immersed in nature. An old-growth maritime hammock houses slash pines and strangler figs. The hammock, one of four habitats in the 436-acre park, also contains cabbage palms, gumbo-limbos, pond apples, and the shady Satinleaf Trail. A second habitat, the estuary, swarms with fish and oysters, and at certain times of the year, manatees lumber through the shallows. An elevated boardwalk leads to the third habitat, the beach and dune. The beach is 1.6 miles of unspoiled coastline shielded from erosion by the dune. The fourth habitat is submerged. Suit up in your mask, snorkel, and fins to see the splendor of the Anastasia limestone rock reef.

10900 Jack Nicklaus Dr., North Palm Beach, 561-624-6950
macarthurbeach.org

LEARN ABOUT
THE LOXAHATCHEE RIVER

The Loxahatchee River Center and its eye-catching exhibits pique the public's interest about the first nationally designated "Wild and Scenic" river in Florida. Depicting different habitats found along the river, the exhibits document how the precious watershed protects its banks. Six thousand gallons of H2O fill multiple aquariums where familiar—and not-so-familiar—finned and footed species flourish. Children love the touch tank that allows them to hold horseshoe crabs, sea urchins, and starfish. The reptile room has corn snakes and lizards crawling around in three terrariums. Interactive displays aim to raise awareness of the health of the natural resource and encourage environmental stewardship. There is a year-round Monthly Lecture Series, which includes lunch, and in the spring and fall months when the weather is pleasant, you can sign up for hikes, kayak trips, seine and dip netting, and other outdoor excursions led by a naturalist.

805 US Hwy. 1, 561-743-7123
lrdrivercenter.org

Palm Beach Gardens banyan tree
Photo courtesy of Amy Woods

CULTURE AND HISTORY

BURN YOUR BUNS
AT THE JUPITER INLET LIGHTHOUSE

Climbing the 105 spiral steps to the top of the Jupiter Inlet Lighthouse will give you one heck of a workout. After regaining your normal heart rate while circling the gallery, come back down to earth and walk the sacred grounds surrounding the red beacon. The 120-acre site, nationally registered as a Bureau of Land Management Outstanding Natural Area, takes visitors through more than 5,000 years of history. Sense the Native American burial ground. See the sizable shell midden. Sit beneath a Seminole Chickee hut. Soak in the stories of the Jeaga and Jobe tribes who fished the Loxahatchee River and hunted its then-bare banks. Guided tours of the Jupiter Inlet Lighthouse, given several times each week, are extensive and last two hours, covering cultural and natural history in addition to military history. Spectacular sunset tours and majestic moonrise tours also are provided.

500 Captain Armour's Way, 561-747-8380
jupiterlighthouse.org

TIP

Any visit to the Jupiter Inlet Lighthouse merits a trip across the street to the Lighthouse Diner. The old comfort-food mainstay shines brightly in full '50s-era glory, its menu beaming with burgers, fries, and shakes, home-cooked meals like chicken pot pie, and a daily Blue Plate Special. Plus, you can order breakfast all day.

1510 N US Hwy. 1, 561-529-2883, lighthousedinerfl.com

BEHOLD THE BARD
AT SHAKESPEARE BY THE SEA

Kick back under the stars on a steamy summer night and savor the singular sensation known as Shakespeare by the Sea. The annual outdoor soiree brings the best of the English playwright's soliloquies and sonnets to the stage, free of charge. Grab your camp chairs and your coolers—yes, alcohol is allowed—and head to the park-like venuc early to secure your spot and partake in a picnic worthy of Henry VIII. Take your children along, too. All content is age-appropriate. Plus, they can run around on the grass prior to curtain call. Your pets can accompany you as well, just be sure to keep them leashed. The locally produced and acted production takes place during two back-to-back weekends in July (eight evenings in all) and attracts tens of thousands of attendees anticipating a thought-provoking performance that always mixes in some modern-day irreverence for fun.

Seabreeze Amphitheater
750 S A1A, 561-762-8552
pbshakespeare.org

TIP

The nonprofit Palm Beach Shakespeare Festival runs Shakespeare by the Sea and encourages guests to make a $5 donation. Funds cover the cost of putting on the play and ensure the more-than-three-decades-old tradition continues. As Portia said in *The Merchant of Venice*, "How far that little candle throws his beams! So shines a good deed in a weary world."

63

LISTEN TO THE WALLS TALK
AT THE SIMS HOUSE

The Mission-style masterwork built in 1924 sits on a street corner in one of Jupiter's first neighborhoods. Designated as a historic structure on an equally historic site, the 2,100-square-foot property is privately owned but publicly accessible. A beautifully maintained two-bedroom, two-and-a-half-bathroom stucco dwelling, it operates as a small restaurant. Dinner is served five nights a week both inside the Dade County pine-laden, living spaces–turned–eating areas and in the expansive back yard. Off to the side, a rustic bar stocked with a dozen beers on tap entices. Inside, you will find an antique piano, vintage furniture, and lots of period décor. The original fireplace is intact, and there is a table for four right in front of it. Even the quaint porch with views of the sidewalk has seating. You will feel as if you are at your grandparents' house for Sunday supper.

322 Center St., 561-431-4336
facebook.com/simshouse1924

RETRACE THE STEPS
OF A GANGSTER

Al Capone, the notorious Chicago mob boss, secretly owned a home near a large tomato field in Jupiter during the Prohibition Era. No, Scarface did not plant seeds or tend crops. Nor did the career criminal live in the remote retreat. Instead, Capone bought the home and the 180 acres surrounding it as a hideout for his known associates. The stash house on what was then named Italian Farms Road is said to have kept some of the outlaw's goons alive and well. Fast-forward to the 1960s, and the plot thickens. The property exchanged hands a couple of times and eventually became Burt Reynolds Ranch, the beloved actor's abode. Reynolds filmed part of *Smokey and the Bandit II* on-site in 1980 and wed Loni Anderson there in 1988. The Town & Country Feed & Supply store now stands in the original structure's place.

16133 Jupiter Farms Rd.

ACE A CLASS
AT FLORIDA ATLANTIC UNIVERSITY

The public college (go Owls!) has a satellite school 40 miles north of its main Boca Raton digs. While the feisty football games go down on the south campus, on the north campus, fans are fired up about the Osher Lifelong Learning Institute's spring, fall, and winter terms. Described as "the college of your dreams," OLLI attracts adult knowledge-seekers who thrive on immersing themselves in university-level classes taught by renowned instructors. Not a drop of homework is assigned, and not a single test is given. Seasoned pupils study a wide variety of subject matter. Past classes have covered art history through the ages, American foreign policy, and the personal lives of US presidents. Lighter fare is offered, too, such as examinations of 21st-century music, 20th-century films, and the comedic stylings of Johnny Carson. FAU's institute is the largest of the 125 OLLI programs countrywide.

5353 Parkside Dr., 561-799-8547
fau.edu/osherjupiter

66

MARCH
TO THE MILITARY TRAIL FLORIDA HERITAGE LANDMARK

Military Trail, a busy surface street that parallels Interstate 95 and Florida's Turnpike, spans some 46 miles from its beginning at Indiantown Road to its terminus in Broward County—Deerfield Beach to be exact. Nearly two centuries have passed since the utilitarian pathway was cut by American soldiers during the Second Seminole War. Maj. William Lauderdale, following orders from Maj. Gen. Thomas Jesup, led the effort. It took troops four days to reach the strategic destination, the north fork of the New River, where a fort was erected. Military Trail officially earned its name during the Third Seminole War. Because of its location on an inland ridge as opposed to coastal wetlands, Army forces used it extensively for operations. An ornate clocktower and a Florida Heritage Landmark sign rise from the trailhead, now a sprawling six-lane intersection surrounded by banks, drug stores, and fast-food restaurants.

Intersection of Indiantown Rd. and Clocktower Dr.

TOUR THE TOWN OF JUPITER
GALLERY OF ART

A free exhibition that changes every few months and promotes the two- and three-dimensional works of local artists is open to the public six days a week. The gallery's generous hours, 8 a.m. to 9 p.m. Mondays through Fridays and 8 a.m. to 4 p.m. Saturdays, give viewers ample time to browse the framed paintings, photographs, and prints along with the bronze, clay, and jeweled creations. All the content is selected by the Town of Jupiter Art Committee for the various shows. A past exhibition titled *With Love* celebrated Valentine's Day and focused on the artists' interpretations of *amore*. The gallery not only generates a forum for homegrown talent but also enlightens those who come to explore. Everything on the walls and in the display cases is for sale. Each exhibition kicks off with an evening reception where you can enjoy refreshments and peruse the merchandise.

Jupiter Community Center
200 Military Trl., 561-746-5134
jupiter.fl.us

68

TRAVEL BACK TO THE TURN OF THE 20TH CENTURY AT THE DUBOIS PIONEER HOME

Harry DuBois married Susan Sanders in 1898 after proposing to the bride-to-be at the top of the Jupiter Inlet Lighthouse. During the romantic moment, the story goes, DuBois noticed a 20-foot-high, 600-foot-long shell mound along the bank of the Loxahatchee River and knew that was where he wanted to build a house and settle down as a newlywed. The DuBois Pioneer Home has endured for more than 200 years and today is open for free, docent-led tours. Listed on the National Register of Historical Places, it exemplifies the lost-to-history homesteads of the era. The DuBoises raised four children in the home, the eldest of whom operated it as a fish camp and seafood restaurant. Located in DuBois Park, managed by Palm Beach County, the site also preserves the archeologically sensitive Native American midden and the ancient tools, treasures, and other artifacts found within it.

19075 DuBois Rd., 561-966-6609
pbcgov.com/parks

69

WATCH PAINT DRY
AT THE *PLEIN AIR* FESTIVAL

While the Lighthouse ArtCenter Gallery & School of Art has outstanding exhibitions year-round—past shows have heralded Hunt Slonem, Andy Warhol, and the Florida Highwaymen—the annual *Plein Air* Festival captures on canvas the reasons to love Jupiter and the surrounding area. A juried event, it draws artists from around the United States for a week of outdoor composition in picturesque parks and preserves. The public is welcome to observe the artists on location as they create their flora- and fauna-filled visuals in real time. If you want to wait until after the paint dries, attend the Collectors' Party & Sale on the final night to mix and mingle, eat and drink, and determine which one of those beauties to buy. Some of the creatives schedule workshops to teach tricks of the trade. The *Plein Air* Festival occurs during the insanely envious weather of March.

373 Tequesta Dr., Tequesta, 561-746-3101
lighthousearts.org

70

PAY YOUR RESPECTS TO THE DEAD
AT RIVERSIDE MEMORIAL PARK

What do Perry Como, Chuck Daly, and Mike Douglas have in common? Besides being household names back in their day, all three are resting in peace at Riverside Memorial Park. Como (1912–2001), the crooner who sang "Catch a Falling Star," "Hot Diggity (Dog Ziggity Boom)," and "Magic Moments," once lived in Jupiter Inlet Colony. Daly (1930–2009) coached the Detroit Pistons to NBA championships in 1989 and 1990 and led the Dream Team to Olympic gold in 1992, eventually retiring to Jupiter. Douglas (1925–2006), the talk show host who had a home in Palm Beach Gardens, entertained television audiences for more than 20 years. One of his most notable episodes featured the first national appearance of Tiger Woods at age two. Also buried at the cemetery is Gary Carter (1954–2012), a crack catcher for the Montreal Expos and the New York Mets who resided in Palm Beach Gardens as well.

19351 SE County Line Rd., Tequesta, 561-747-1100
dignitymemorial.com

STIMULATE YOUR RIGHT BRAIN
AT ARTFEST BY THE SEA AT JUNO BEACH

The annual showcase has a geographical advantage no other festival of its kind does. Situated on A1A, or as the locals call it, the beach road, the much-looked-forward-to affair stretches roughly one mile along the two-lane oceanfront drive lined with sea grape trees that lead down to the dune. Breathing in the refreshing salt air will alter your mood. As for the goods, they range from delicately beaded pieces of jewelry to larger-than-life metal sculptures to everything in between—ceramics, drawings, fiber work, and photography. Both the environmental and esoteric aspects of ArtFest by the Sea at Juno Beach combine to make the designated weekend in March visually euphoric not only for patrons but also for the more than 250 artists displaying their wares. Organized by the Palm Beach North Chamber of Commerce, the event is free and has a convenient shuttle service.

561-746-7111
artfestbythesea.com

72

ADMIRE THE AGAM AT THE MANDEL JEWISH COMMUNITY CENTER

An incredible optical illusion of a sculpture bursting with color fortifies the Mandel Jewish Community Center in Palm Beach Gardens. The work of internationally acclaimed artist Yaacov Agam, the 10-foot-tall, nine-panel-wide, geometric spectacle has graced the grounds since 1993. A Palestinian-born Israel resident, Agam visited the campus to supervise the installation of *Menorah* and dedicate it with his signature. Local philanthropist Harriet Miller funded the piece by making a donation to the JCC; the gesture honored Miller's husband Alan in recognition of his 60th birthday. *Menorah* richly represents the breakthrough lenticular style that defines the Agam aesthetic. Its imagery changes depending on where you stand and continues to change when you view it from different angles. Originating from an oil painting by Agam that has hung at the center since it first opened in 1989 in West Palm Beach, the metal masterpiece must be mused.

5221 Hood Rd., Palm Beach Gardens, 561-712-5200
pbg.jcconline.com

TIP

Menorah is disassembled every June and put into storage to keep it safe during hurricane season. It is reassembled in early December. Please plan accordingly!

73

BRUSH UP ON THE BACKGROUND
OF THE BANYAN TREE

At the official entrance to Palm Beach Gardens stands a big, branched beauty whose lush foliage forms a tall canopy welcoming all to the city. The *ficus benghalensis*'s aerial roots give an artistic appearance to the more-than-century-old specimen. Dozens of blooming peace lilies surround it in a specially engineered median. Had it not been for the efforts of city founder and visionary John D. MacArthur, the banyan tree would not exist. Upon hearing it was slated for removal in a neighboring community, MacArthur decided to have all 75 tons of it transported across town via crane. Since 1961, the towering timber, united with a second, smaller banyan tree in 1962, has served as the city's symbol and is a focal point on the city's emblem. A Historic Banyan Trees Florida Heritage Site marker and two benches offer an opportunity for passive reflection on the gorgeous green goddess.

Intersection of Northlake and MacArthur Boulevards, Palm Beach Gardens

TIP

Lake Catherine Park, named after John D. MacArthur's wife, is a quick and easy walk from the banyan tree. The park has a loop trail good for bicycling and running, provides pretty views of the water, and is flush with flora. The Palm Beach Gardens Woman's Club plants a statement tree in the park every year on Arbor Day with signage identifying the species. Walk beneath the royal poinciana, smell the Southern magnolia, and gaze at the white geiger to experience a living gallery.

9481 MacArthur Blvd., Palm Beach Gardens
561-804-7034, pbgfl.com

LAY YOUR EYES ON A 1940 AMERICAN LAFRANCE

AT THE PETER T. BERGEL FIRE MUSEUM

Few fire departments have their original engine. Palm Beach Gardens is one of them. Shiny and spiffy, the lovingly restored 1940 American LaFrance shelters in the building that housed the city's first volunteer squad. The building, a former garage of a private home, operated as the rallying point for firefighters when an alarm sounded. In 1963, a staffed department took over the space. All the while, the bright red 500 Series Pumper answered calls. When the Palm Beach Gardens Municipal Campus opened at the corner of Burns Road and Military Trail, the garage was moved, renovated, and later dedicated as The Peter T. Bergel Fire Museum. Old turnout coats, an antique oxygen tank, and a handwritten logbook are among the relics on display. The 1940 American LaFrance no longer responds to emergencies, but it runs like a champ and makes appearances at area fairs and festivals.

4425 Burns Rd., Palm Beach Gardens, 561-799-4300
pbgfl.com

PONDER PIECES
IN THE ART IN PUBLIC PLACES PROGRAM

A Palm Beach Gardens ordinance requiring private developers to include publicly accessible artwork in their projects has residents stumbling upon unexpected objects throughout the city. At Shoppes of Oakbrook, a tortoise crouches in the courtyard. Nearby, an eagle is about to take flight. At Palm Beach Gardens Medical Center, a pair of Key deer forage the grounds. Thomas Jefferson sits on a bench in Mirasol Town Square, quill pen in hand. The Florida-themed carousel at Downtown Palm Beach Gardens, a functional piece of art that gives rides daily, offers children the choice of a flamingo, a manatee, a seahorse, and two dozen other animals to sit on and take a spin. The merry-go-round amusement also depicts local history, beach scenes, and several types of flowers including desert rose, gardenia, and hibiscus. The most famous piece in the Art in Public Places program, *Astralis* comprises four round steel forms that illuminate the PGA Boulevard flyover.

561-799-4243
pbgfl.com

STROLL DOWN MEMORY LANE

AT THE PALM BEACH GARDENS HISTORICAL SOCIETY

Incorporated in 1959, Palm Beach Gardens has a colorful history as a city that embodied the "go green" movement before the "go green" movement trended. It began with a Chicago insurance magnate who had a vision of a flourishing community filled with fields, parks, and open space. John D. MacArthur swiftly snapped up thousands of acres of scrubland and appealed to the Florida Legislature for the establishment of a "garden city." A brash billionaire with an eccentric character, MacArthur had much the same impact on mid-20th-century Palm Beach County as railroad king Henry Flagler had on turn-of-the-19th-century Palm Beach County. The Palm Beach Gardens Historical Society documents MacArthur's legacy (he died in 1978 at age 80) and displays an interesting collection of carefully curated memorabilia, newspaper clippings, photos, and other items for the public to view.

3950 RCA Blvd., Palm Beach Gardens, 561-799-4100
pbghistory.org

TIP

The society's location is historical as well. The office in suite 5050 sits deep within a divergent business park known as the NorthCorp Center where workers once assembled electronics for the Radio Corporation of America, or RCA. The plant dates back to 1961.

CHAT WITH ARTISTS FROM ACROSS THE COUNTRY

AT ARTIGRAS

Its name is carved into the Presidents' Day Weekend calendar, and for good reason. ArtiGras, a popular and prestigious fine-art festival, features a registry of 300 painters, potters, sculptors, and others who staff their booths for two days selling things of beauty. Other mediums include glass and wood, with jewelry makers and digital artists rounding out the offerings. The sheer quality of the workmanship has launched ArtiGras into the upper echelon of juried art shows nationwide. The wonderful winter weather (think sunny and 75) adds to the enjoyment of finding the perfect piece to take home and love. So does the live music, gourmet food, and creative cocktail called ArtiPunch. Why not treat yourself like a VIP by scoring tickets to the hospitality tent? The exclusive area serves complimentary bites and beverages and is a place to rest and regroup. You will need it—the festival encompasses nearly 12 acres.

Gardens North County District Park
5101 117th Ct. N, Palm Beach Gardens, 561-746-7111
artigras.org

78

MAKE A STOP ON THE FLORIDA HISTORIC GOLF TRAIL

AT THE NORTH PALM BEACH COUNTRY CLUB

In 1926, well-known golf course architect and engineer Seth Raynor designed the links at the North Palm Beach Country Club, then called the Palm Beach Winter Club. A warm-weather destination for the rich and famous living on the posh island, the club was acquired by the village in 1962 and renamed. Since then, the course has undergone a few redesigns, the most recent by the legendary Jack Nicklaus, a longtime resident. One of two trademarked Jack Nicklaus Signature courses in the United States, it demands skill and strategy to make successful lies and avoid the natural sand dunes. In 2019, *Golf* magazine ranked it as one of the top 30 municipal courses in America. It now joins more than 50 courses from the Keys to the Panhandle that not only are publically playable but also highlight the heritage of the game in the state.

951 US Hwy. 1, North Palm Beach, 561-691-3433
floridahistoricgolftrail.com

79

SUPPORT SMALL THEATER AT THE PALM BEACH INSTITUTE FOR THE ENTERTAINMENT ARTS

What remains of the Burt Reynolds Institute for Theatre Training, debuting in 1979, and the Burt Reynolds Institute for Film and Theatre, debuting in 1999, found a home at the Palm Beach Institute for the Entertainment Arts. Bits of movie memorabilia fill the small black-box studio still mourning the loss of its former namesake. The nonprofit carries on Reynolds's mission of helping aspiring actors to find their place on the stage, educating working actors through coursework, and furthering the careers of professional actors via advanced classes. The concept theater's productions are affordably priced and deliver lots of laughs. One such production, Guerilla Theatre, adds a local spin that leaves audiences in stitches after they watch a series of unrehearsed scenes and spontaneous performances with surprises at every turn. Get your tickets to see original plays, evening concerts, movie matinees, and more.

115 US Hwy. 1, North Palm Beach, 561-743-9955
pbinstituteforentertainmentarts.com

STAND ON THE SITE OF THE SECOND SEMINOLE WAR

AT LOXAHATCHEE RIVER BATTLEFIELD PARK

A 61-acre swath of land preserved by Palm Beach County as Loxahatchee River Battlefield Park saw a lot of action during the Second Seminole War. Two significant fights occurred in January of 1838, nine days apart, as the American offensive to remove the Florida tribe from its reservation ensued. The first Battle of the Loxahatchee was named after Lt. Levin Powell, with the second named after Maj. Gen. Thomas Jesup. Both begat the Third Seminole War, a series of skirmishes from 1855 to 1858 that ended the conflict. As you meander the trails traversing tree-lined flatwoods and grassy meadows, it is difficult to imagine that blood was shed on such glorious grounds. The Loxahatchee Battlefield Preservationists, a group of volunteers who formed a nonprofit to protect the park, gives weekly tours, organizes a seasonal lecture series, and stages an annual two-day Battle of the Loxahatchee reenactment.

9060 W Indiantown Rd., 561-741-1359
pbcgov.com/parks

Fishing rods and reels and
sports memorabilia at Man Cave
Photo courtesy of Geoffrey Gilroy

SHOPPING AND FASHION

SPEND AN EVENING
AT THE ABACOA GREEN MARKET

Most green markets get underway at the crack of dawn, during oh-dark-hundred, in the wee small hours, etc. If you are not an early riser and prefer to hit the snooze button repeatedly on that pesky alarm clock, the Abacoa Green Market is calling your name. The same fresh finds available at the morning markets (baked goods, organic produce, roasted coffees, spiced teas, and truffle oils) await you between 5 and 8 p.m. Wednesdays. Some of the 40-something vendors set up around the amphitheater sell infused cocktail mixes, preservative-free dog treats, tarot cards, and tie-dye T-shirts plus candles, crafts, soaps, plants, and tinctures. The event takes place in the height of the South Florida season (October through May) and has live music on tap. Afterward, you can get a table at one of the many nearby restaurants and make a night of it.

Abacoa Town Center
1260 University Blvd., 561-254-5120
abacoagreenmarket.com

FOR THOSE WHO THRIVE ON WAKING UP WITH THE SUN, HERE ARE TWO MORNING MARKETS WHERE YOU CAN RISE AND SHINE

JoJo's Farmers Market
A monthly market, it runs from 9 a.m. to 2 p.m. select Saturdays in Carlin Park.
750 S A1A, 954-240-3443
jojosfarmersmarket.com/jupiter

The Gardens GreenMarket
From 8 a.m. to 1 p.m. Sundays, more than 100 vendors tend their booths at the Palm Beach Gardens Municipal Campus.
10500 N Military Trl., Palm Beach Gardens, 561-630-1100
pbgfl.com

LOL
AT GRETCHEN SCOTT

The eccentric entrepreneur whose eponymous clothing boutique epitomizes fun in the sun has a blast coming up with names for her playful patterns and prints: Flamingle and Frond Frenzy, Magic Carpet and Mystic Garden, Sea of Love and Sea Sway. A detailed description of the who, what, when, where, why, and how behind the inspiration accompanies each design. Hummingbird Heaven evolved from watching the colorful wing flappers feed on trumpet vines. Neptune's Playground portrays the beneath-your-feet view on a glass-bottom boat ride. Paisley Paradise's curious shapes derive from the Far East while Tassel Time's feathery knots were sparked by their use in draperies and rugs. The list goes on. Gretchen Scott's original caftans and embroidered tunics symbolize the brand. Purchase one tunic in particular—Turtle Tides—and all proceeds will benefit the Loggerhead Marinelife Center, an ocean conservancy and turtle hospital in Juno Beach.

287 E Indiantown Rd., 561-746-3199
gretchenscottdesigns.com

GO COASTAL
AT JUNO SHOE GIRL

Here, your flip-flops feature free bling. Every pair sold comes with a dazzling set of ornaments of your choice. Pick from pink anchors or gold crabs. Hem and haw between orange hibiscus flowers and silver sand dollars. If you are a sporty diva, try ornaments with tennis racquets or golf clubs on them. No matter what you decide, your cork slides, embossed flats, or patent platforms will look all dressed up for either day or night. At Juno Shoe Girl, not only do the sandals tempt but so do the handcrafted jewelry, one-of-a-kind totes, and other beachy goods that ignite beachy passions. The store's designers named the boutique after the ancient mythological goddess Juno, believed to have wed Jupiter and given birth to Mars. Juno is said to be a protector of women, encouraging them to embody their own spirit and individual beauty.

318 US Hwy. 1, 561-320-9311
junoshoegirl.com

DRAG YOUR KNUCKLES
TO MAN CAVE

Guys, you cannot visit Jupiter without a trip to this testosterone-drenched store. Trust me, you will be happy you did. As you browse the macho-esque merchandise (think taxidermy animal mounts, fishing rods and reels, sports memorabilia, and, of course, power tools), do not be surprised if the owner hands you a beer from the refrigerator. Go with it. The business operates on a consignment basis and works with hundreds of community members looking to sell their stuff. Inventory changes frequently, so you never know what kind of dude-friendly deal you are going to find. Have you always longed for a vintage poker table or an oversize leather chair or nostalgic records to hang on the wall? Man Cave has it all within its 3,000 square feet of territory in an old industrial park. It is a one-stop shop for everything your loving spouse will not buy you.

1665 N Old Dixie Hwy., 561-746-2283
mancaveconsign.com

TIP

Does your taste lean more toward cosmopolitan than caveman? At True Treasures, you will find yourself standing upright as you shop the meticulously inspected merchandise that puts quality above quantity.

111 US Hwy. 1, North Palm Beach and 3918 Northlake Blvd., Palm Beach Gardens, 561-625-9569, truetreasuresinc.com

ENJOY THE HUNT AND LEAVE YOUR WOODEN CLUB AT HOME. GO THRIFTING AT ANY OF THE BUSINESSES LISTED BELOW FOR A BARGAIN

Furry Friends Thrift Boutique
615 W Indiantown Rd., 561-747-5311 or 561-529-4075
furryfriendsadoption.org/thrift-boutique

Jupiter Medical Center Thrift Shop
205 Center St., 561-746-1601
jupitermed.com/patients-visitors/facilities-amenities/thrift-shop

Quantum House Resale Shop
800 W Indiantown Rd., 561-290-0316
quantumhouse.org/resale-shop

Hospice of Palm Beach County Resale Shop
863 Donald Ross Rd., Juno Beach, 561-624-5495
trustbridge.com/foundation/ways-to-give/resale-shops

DROP IN
ON A GNARLY SURF SHOP

Paddling out, popping up, and taking off could be considered core curriculum in Jupiter. The town's five-mile-long shoreline has a decent groundswell and year-round warm waters ideal for surfing. Locals Surf Shop, a family-owned boardsports business, caters to the catch-a-wave community while also offering a totally tubular experience to someone shopping for T-shirts, cut-offs, and a pair of thongs, to quote The Beach Boys's song "All Summer Long". The store sells threads for men, women, and children, bitchin' beach bags, tasty towels with the emblematic Locals logo on them, and other cool stuff like magnets, keychains, and air fresheners—the kind that dangle from a string around your rearview mirror. Nothing says "cowabunga" like a stick of Sun Bum tinted lip balm in the subtle shade of Nude Beach or the not-so-subtle shade of Raisin Hell. And check this out: a Locals Shaved Ice stand within the store scoops out a frosty feast of flavors including Bahama Mama, Pink Bubble Gum, and Tutti Frutti.

4050 US Hwy. 1, 561-624-6006
localssurfshop.com

TIP

Get stoked about another Jupiter surf shop, Ocean Magic, whose original 5,000-square-foot location has served the Barneys and Bettys of the area since 1986. In 2022, the new owners opened a second location in The Gardens Mall, providing all the gadgets and gear needed for an endless summer.

103 S US Hwy. 1, Ste. C6, 561-744-8925
3101 PGA Blvd., Palm Beach Gardens, 561-425-5436
oceanmagicsurf.com

FIND YOUR FLORIDA FLAIR
AT ANTHONY'S

A sartorial staple in the Sunshine State, Anthony's will have you looking like a Florida girl in no time. With 12 locations across the peninsula, the store's flagship is nestled in an old shopping center where brand-loyal followers flock. Are you pining for a pair of pants with palm fronds on them or searching for a starfish-print skort? How about a blouse brimming with sea creatures or a pineapple-festooned summer sweater? Is a striped monstera leaf dress missing from your closet? The sunny style of the 128-year-old-and-counting business famous for its easy, breezy "Ladies Apparel" sets it apart from other resort-wear retailers. Believe it or not, three men were behind the fashion favorite. The Anthony brothers, Gus, James, and Emile, opened it in 1895, one year before Henry Flagler's Florida East Coast Railway reached Miami. Anthony's still is family owned and operated today.

4300 US Hwy. 1, 561-277-9808
anthonysfla.com

87

UNDERSTAND WHAT THOSE WITH AUTISM CAN DO
AT THE CHOCOLATE SPECTRUM

Every confection, cup of coffee, and piece of pastry at The Chocolate Spectrum has a story behind it. The up-and-coming chocolatiers, baristas, and pastry chefs who prepare each of the products have autism. The adult son of the store's founder is one of them. When Valerie Herskowitz began teaching Blake, who was diagnosed at age two, how to mold candy, it transformed him into someone who, for at least a few hours of the day, did not need around-the-clock care. Herskowitz opened the nonprofit business to help others on the spectrum. She succeeded. Upward of 50 trainees have gained meaningful skills that bring a sense of purpose to their lives. The Chocolate Spectrum also employs some of its students to run the café and retail operation. Customers who purchase sweets in turn support the cause as all proceeds from sales go toward funding the program.

6725 W Indiantown Rd., Ste. 38, 561-277-9886
thechocolatespectrum.com

BOOT-SCOOT OUT
OF J. C. WESTERN WEAR

Whether you are a two-stepper or a tourist, the oldest apparel store of its kind in Florida will outfit you in cowboy boots so country they will make men swagger and women sashay. Select your heel and toe style from Ariat, Corral, Durango, Lucchese, and other big names with as much or as little flare as you want. Female embellishments include embroidered overlays, faux fur, and metal studs. For the men, slip on a black harness boot with a strider heel and a square toe or maybe a saddle-brown boot with the state flag emblazoned on the shaft. Way more than boots are for sale at J. C. Western Wear. Check out the blue denim or fringed suede jackets and hats of felt and straw. Branch out with bandanas, belt buckles, and bolo ties. And if you are feeling adventurous, invest in a braided bullwhip or a pair of "spurs that jingle jangle jingle" to complete the look.

710 N Old Dixie Hwy., 561-748-8801
jcwesternwear.com

SQUEEZE EVERY DROP
OUT OF TERMARSCH GROVES

Bags, bins, and bundles of fresh Florida citrus have drawn customers from all over the map to the family-owned fruit stand for 64 years and counting. Known for its tangy Ruby Red grapefruits, bright Glory Orri mandarins, odd-shaped Honeybell tangelos, and rich Navel oranges, TerMarsch Groves has gained serious street cred as a roadside attraction. Its eclectically imaginative gift shop has no shortage of Sunshine State kitsch (think alligator heads, mermaid statues, plastic flamingos, and shells galore) tastefully rounded out by jarred jams and jellies, jugged juices, and specialty sweets like coconut patties and key lime cookies. All-natural ice cream fills the freezer, and gourmet pies are baked to order. Souvenir hats and tie-dye T-shirts appeal to the men, cute couture and pretty jewelry appeal to the women. While you look around, you will be offered a complimentary cup of just-squeezed OJ.

13900 US Hwy. 1, Juno Beach, 561-626-1177
shipfloridaoranges.com

TIP

A short distance south of TerMarsch Groves is another go-to for fresh fruits—and vegetables. At The Yankee Peddler Produce & Market, you will find a selection of gourmet foods, deli items, and sweet and savory goods baked to perfection.

12174 US Hwy. 1, Juno Beach, 561-629-7703, ypproduce.com

SEARCH FOR SOMETHING SPECIAL AT EXCENTRICITIES

The whimsical wares at the high-end home-décor store speak of salty, sandy days and warm, windy nights by the water. The panorama of pieces Excentricities sells ranges from artwork to pillows, from lamps to tables, and from cabinets to club chairs. Every item conveys a fresh whiff of the ocean, the rolling sound of a wave, and rum-spiked sips of boat drinks. The bright and cheery showroom basks in a blue colorway: Corals, florals, and fronds in navy, powder, and royal appear on the fabric coverings of soft goods; blue herons, blue seas, and blue skies are the subjects of most of the framed paintings and prints. Light fixtures are composed of driftwood, glass, and shells. The furniture is simple and streamlined, befitting of a beach bungalow or a cottage on the coast. Whatever you select, it will perennially remind you of your Floridays.

225 E Indiantown Rd., 561-748-5440
excentricities.com

TIP

You also can search for something special at Patrick Day Home Gallery. Goods from the far reaches of the globe stuff a showroom spanning 10,000 square feet that will have your head swiveling amid the sheer abundance.

1226 W Indiantown Rd., 561-748-0282
patrickdayhome.com

91

DIG THE EARTHY ESSENCE
OF HERBS & OWLS

Alfalfa can help reduce cholesterol, flush out toxins, and improve digestion. Moringa fights inflammation, eases symptoms of menopause, and nourishes the skin. Turmeric is touted for treating headaches and lowering the risk of viral infections. All three organic herbs, and hundreds of other medicinal barks, flowers, powders, and roots, are sold by the ounce at an out-of-the-box boutique owned and operated by a registered herbalist. Herbs & Owls (the owl symbolizes wisdom) takes your holistic journey a step further by letting you book a spiritual shamanic healing session, buy a stress-relieving sound-therapy package, or schedule a private consultation to put you on a path to better health through alternative practices. Shop for crystals to address your chakras, pick up some smudges for burning rituals, or peruse self-help publications. You can take a community class on meditation methods, the benefits of qigong, how to blend tea leaves, and more.

725 N A1A, Ste. D-103, 561-768-9005
herbsandowls.com

TAKE THE FORK IN THE ROAD
AT JUNO BEACH MART

Wedged between US Highway 1 and A1A, Juno Beach Mart earned its way onto the *100 Things* list by setting the bar for gas stations across the country. When you pull into the spotless bay, you will start to smile at the Americana you see in every direction. The Dad's Root Beer thermometer. An old-fashioned Mobilgas pump. That handsome dimpled man on a Richfield Oil sign. As you get out of your car, you hear music that turns the chore of filling up your tank into a surprisingly pleasant experience. While you wait, you can check out the finely restored black-and-red Ford pickup, its driver door advertising the Texaco star logo. Need to use the restroom? It is air-conditioned and clean. If you enter the convenience store, you will be tempted to buy a cold bottle of Coca-Cola from the antique vending machine or a box of 1950s-era candy.

12750 US Hwy. 1, 561-622-6885
facebook.com/people/juno-beach-mobil/100054466509955

JUMP INTO A PAIR OF JACK ROGERS AT VILLAGE BOOTERY

The iconic sandals owe their existence to Jackie Kennedy. The fashionable first lady returned from a trip to Capri with a pair of whipstitched thongs in tow. Mrs. Kennedy fell in love with the Italian workmanship and wanted to replicate the style back home, so she brought them to a shoemaker on Palm Beach, and the rest is history. The iconic brand debuted in 1960. In 1962, Village Bootery opened 25 miles north of the Winter White House. Today, the shoe store still is going strong not only because it has three generations of loyal customers but also because it carries the largest collection of Jack Rogers in the area. The original Navajo style that started it all comes in a palette of preppy colors. The Georgica Jelly does, too. A recent addition to the line, the Comfort Jacks have a thicker sole for those who live in their sandals, dawn to dusk.

245 S US Hwy. 1, Tequesta, 561-467-7768
villagebootery.com

TIP

Slip on your new shoes and break them in by walking a few doors down to Hog Snappers, a sushi shack and seafood joint in the same shopping center as Village Bootery. The scratch kitchen prepares everything in house from the clam chowder to the crab cakes to the crostini.

279 S US Hwy. 1, Tequesta
561-401-9309, hogsnappersshackandsushi.com

SCHEDULE A STYLING APPOINTMENT AT EVELYN & ARTHUR

Have you had a good look lately? Even if your answer to the contemporary clothing store's slogan is yes, block out some you time for a session with a personal shopper. Visit the Evelyn & Arthur website, scroll to the bottom where it says, "Get Styled," and select a time and date. The half-hour VIP treatment will awaken the fashionista in you. A bountiful boutique, it prides itself on flirty and fun interpretations of age-appropriate clothing for women. Upon entering the glass doors, you will encounter a lively lifestyle table showing off the store's top-trending merchandise. As you admire the handbags, jewelry, and other accessories along with a few ready-to-wear outfits artfully displayed, a sales representative will greet you. Then, prepare to be taken away to wardrobe-land. If you prefer to shop incognito, stop in any day of the week.

10937 Military Trl., Palm Beach Gardens, 561-572-0900
evelynandarthur.com

95

WALK
THE GARDENS MALL

More than 1.4 million square feet of marbled floors house 140 of the finest retailers in the region, anchored by Bloomingdale's and Saks Fifth Avenue to the north and Macy's to the south. One of six locations statewide with bragging rights to a Nordstrom, The Gardens Mall's magnificent spread of stores stands out as the premiere shopping destination in northern Palm Beach County. Women's clothing is at the forefront of a well-rounded directory, although men's fashion is more than just a footnote. TravisMathew, with its celebrity sports ambassadors and models, presents a male lifestyle brand that can be worn at work and at play. Robert Graham's rock 'n' roll-ish patterns and prints are way-out-there works of art. Psycho Bunny gives a cutting-edge twist to the conventional collared shirt. The mall's many athletic stores, including Fit2Run and Lululemon, meet the demand of South Florida's body-conscious population.

3101 PGA Blvd., Palm Beach Gardens, 561-775-7750
thegardensmall.com

SWEEP YOURSELF OUT TO SEA
AT OCEANS ALLURE

Throughout the salt-inspired shop, you will encounter sand dollars, starfish, and other underwater wonders lurking in the clothing racks, on the jewelry stands, and atop the accessory-filled tables. The delightful décor-and-more store sells candles and frames, hats and sunglasses, belts and shoes, bath and body items, collars and leashes for your precious pooch, and plush animals and other children's gifts. What differentiates its merchandise from other boutiques is that everything is drenched in a deep-blue-sea theme. Women will find atypical apparel in the collections of palazzos, rompers, ponchos, and kimonos. Looking for a bikini so you can soak up the sun? Take your pick of stringy or strappy. How about a dress for those balmy, breezy nights? Choose a fringed mini, a ruffled midi, or a pleated maxi. Locally owned and locally sourced, Oceans Allure will bring out the beach beauty in you.

Legacy Place
11300 Legacy Ave., Palm Beach Gardens, 561-339-2720
oceansallure.com

97

DELIGHT IN THE DIVERSITY OF ALTON TOWN CENTER

The 344,000-square-foot shopping center rises at the intersection of Donald Ross Road and Interstate 95, the primary entrance to one of Palm Beach Gardens's newer communities. Supporting residents and other neighborhoods, Alton Town Center thrives on a carefully selected mix of tenants. Its retail categories range from beauty and wellness to fashion and accessories, and its pillar is Publix, the prized supermarket synonymous with the state. In the beauty and wellness category, Buff City Soap whips up wonderfully scented, plant-based bars in fun shapes and sizes that lack one thing: chemicals. In the fashion and accessories category, Bergman Jewelers specializes in diamonds and watches and has been locally run for more than four decades. One of the dining and drinking options is a rarity in these parts—a Swedish-American restaurant with five distinct seating areas and Beef Rydberg and Wallenbergare on the menu.

5320 Donald Ross Rd., Palm Beach Gardens, 561-578-8780
altontowncenter.com

PUT ON A PIECE OF PUERTO RICO
AT LOLA CHIQ BOUTIQUE

Two fashion-forward sisters opened their sassy women's store in 2011, recreating a Caribbean island look for flirty Florida females. Whatever the occasion, Maria and Marietta Mercado offer dresses and coordinating shoes, bags, and jewelry to fit the bill. Lola Chiq Boutique has a line of couture and accessories that the two personally select, personally like, and personally would wear, whether to a Monday morning meeting or on a Friday evening date. They curate the goods from Puerto Rico and parts of Spain and bring much-sought-after design options to South Florida's growing Latin community. The shop has another hook as well—every article of clothing it sells costs less than $100. Add one-on-one customer service to the mix of handpicked, well-priced ensembles, and you will begin to plan where you are going to show off your new outfit.

Downtown Palm Beach Gardens
11701 Lake Victoria Gardens Ave., Palm Beach Gardens, 561-629-7786
lolachiq.com

TIP

A half dozen dandelions designed by Dan Shaughnessy IV, whose artistic acronym is DSIV, decorate the breezeway at Downtown Palm Beach Gardens. Titled *The Blooms*, the curious sculptures glisten in the sun during the day and, at night, light up with pulsating LEDs triggered by pedestrian movement.

99

SPOIL YOUR SOLES
AT SANARES SHOES

With 30 years of experience in shoe repair, Sanares Shoes still is the place to find a modern-day cobbler who can masterfully mend leather footwear. But it smartly has capitalized on its reputation as the local go-to for quick fixes for your kicks. Now, an expansive boutique fronts the workroom, welcoming women with its splashy showing of shoes in every shape and size. Boots, heels, and wedges fill the floating shelves on the walls, the decorative stands on the floor, and the old-fashioned window display visible from the sidewalk. Adorable summer sandals, wearable well beyond—and well before—June, July, and August in these parts, sell for as little as $25. Higher-end brands, namely Azura, L'Artiste, and Patrizia, sell for more. The offerings focus on a combination of comfort and beauty, ensuring you will find the perfect pair that fits your feet and your finances.

904 Northlake Blvd., North Palm Beach, 561-844-0830
sanaresshoes.com

CRUISE THROUGH AN OPEN-AIR OASIS BY THE WATER
AT HARBOURSIDE PLACE

Commanding a coveted corner of town ringed by the river, Harbourside Place flaunts clothiers with charisma, a contemporary art gallery, and sweeping views of the Loxahatchee. John Craig, a Florida brand, specializes in menswear and consistently is ranked by fashion magazines as a top purveyor of apparel and accessories for the sophisticated man. Jofit's flagship store sells a line of flattering and functional female athletic wear rooted in the sport of golf. Artlantic has a studio that opens to the public a couple of days each week for interactive experiences with local artists. Harbourside Place's collection of restaurants gives shoppers a chance to refuel, and the marina provides parking for those traveling by boat. The amphitheater, when not used for yoga classes, movie nights, or car shows, has live bands that fill the plaza with music. The dazzling destination is both creatively designed and colorfully painted.

200 N US Hwy. 1, 561-935-9533
harboursideplace.com

Mahalo underway
Photo courtesy of Adam Byerly

ACTIVITIES
BY SEASON

SPRING

SUMMER

FALL

WINTER

SUGGESTED ITINERARIES

TROPICAL ESCAPES

CELEBRITY HAUNTS

ADVENTURES ON THE WATER

DATE NIGHT

FAMILY-FRIENDLY

Wear Your Wet Bathing Suit at Cathy's Beach Connection, 26

Track Turtles at Loggerhead Marinelife Center, 72

Paint a Piece of Pottery at Craft Haus, 50

Behold the Bard at Shakespeare by the Sea, 83

Welcome the Holidays in South Florida Style at the Palm Beach Holiday Boat Parade, 35

Meet the Cast of Characters at Busch Wildlife Sanctuary, 55

See Food and Eat It at the Jupiter Seafood Festival, 19

Play Putt-Putt at Lighthouse Cove Adventure Golf, 58

Marvel at the Motion of the Ocean at Blowing Rocks Preserve, 71

Learn about the Loxahatchee River, 79

EVENTS AND FESTIVALS

Party for the Pooches at the Friends of Jupiter Beach Food & Wine Festival, 4

Watch Paint Dry at the *Plein Air* Festival, 90

See Food and Eat It at the Jupiter Seafood Festival, 19

Festeggiare All Things Italian at the Feast of Little Italy, 29

Chat with Artists from across the Country at ArtiGras, 100

Test Your Luck at the Jupiter Irish Fest, 40

Welcome the Holidays in South Florida Style at the Palm Beach Holiday Boat Parade, 35

Behold the Bard at Shakespeare by the Sea, 83

Stimulate Your Right Brain at ArtFest by the Sea at Juno Beach, 92

Rush the Ropes at the Honda Classic, 76

Solid Brass, a Chicago tribute band, performs at Carlin Park After Dark. Photo courtesy of Valentina Mantilla

INDEX